THE MATH AND LOGIC OF PSYCHOLOGY

Russell Hasan

CONTENTS

INTRODUCTION

This book is a collection of two of my books: On Forgiveness, and To Be Loved, Love. They go together nicely, so I have arranged them in this single edition for your enjoyment.

ON FORGIVENESS

INTRODUCTION

This is an essay on forgiveness, not in the religious sense, but in a purely secular meaning, as in, when one person forgives another person for something they did wrong. The primary focus is on self-forgiveness, where a person forgives themselves, a concept which this essay explains as "moral bankruptcy," using debts and credits and bankruptcy and economics and finance as a metaphor for the moral debts and moral credits that you owe to yourself and to others, that you owe it to yourself to be a good person, and you owe it to other people to be good to them, and, where you fail, you owe them a debt. The human brain evolved in such a way that humans tend to subconsciously seek to repay moral debts through the infliction of emotional pain, either inflicting emotional pain upon the self for debts owed to self (guilt), inflicting pain upon the self for debts owed to others (shame), or inflicting pain upon others for debts they owe to you (anger). This essay, despite being atheistic and secular in nature, does explore forgiveness in the context of areas that are commonly thought of as religious sins: lust, greed, pride, envy, and evil, as well as shame and guilt. The key central idea is that self-forgiveness, "moral bankruptcy," can help set you free from any guilt, shame, and anger that is holding you back in your life, and forgiveness will enable you to live a happier life, by giving you the confidence to act, and to achieve, with a greater resistance to fear of feeling guilt or shame if you fail, thereby tranquilizing fear of rejection or fear of failure or fear of disappointment. This theory of emotions will define honor, emotional maturity, self-esteem, and confidence, as well as explaining all of the seven major emotions: happiness, sadness, love, fear, guilt, shame, and anger. This book is cold, logical, no-nonsense wisdom about forgiveness, and is not mere wishy-washy empty generalities like most self-help books.

MORAL BANKRUPTCY

In The Genealogy of Morals, Friedrich Nietzsche put forward a theory of emotions which I refer to as emotional capitalism. If one of your friends or loved ones owes you a moral debt, and does not repay in kind, you may exact payment by being mean and nasty to them. If you owe them a moral debt, you can repay by being nice to them, or by letting them be mean to you. If someone owes you, you may seek their feelings and expressions of gratitude to pay the debt, or inflict emotional pain to recover your debt. Emotional capital is the debts and credits you owe, or are perceived to owe, to the people in your life.

Emotions can be explained in this way: you feel guilt if you owe a moral debt to someone else to give them your pain in order to pay off your debt. You feel shame if you owe a moral debt for failing social norms or if you owe a debt to society, again, to give your suffering to your creditor as payment. And you feel anger toward someone if they owe you a moral debt which they are not repaying, to extract what you owe from them by getting pain from them when you cause pain to them.

For example, say that you feel you have been a good employee for several years and you deserve a promotion, and your boss passed you over for a promotion and promotes someone else instead. You might get angry at your boss, because, either consciously or subconsciously, you desire to cause your boss pain equal to the moral debt that your boss owed you when he wronged you. Obviously to get angry in this way would be a great way to get fired from your job and lose your salary and ruin your life. Later it will be shown how forgiveness, implemented as moral bankruptcy and emotional maturity, would enable you to forgive your boss, and be a happy productive employee at work.

This theory takes its most interesting turn with the idea that, when you owe something to yourself and fail to obtain it, you owe to yourself a debt you cannot repay, which you must then pay to yourself by inflicting pain and punishment upon yourself: this is the theory of emotional guilt. Moving forward this essay will frequently refer to guilt as the self-inflicted pain of a debt owed to self, and refer to shame as a debt owed to others, although there are some nuances and wrinkles in these definitions. Later it will become clear that shame usually causes guilt to go with it, because you let yourself down by not being good enough for the others whom you sought to impress, and, for this reason, guilt and shame can function as one entity in reality.

From here we finally see the groundwork laid for a theory of moral bankruptcy. In legal bankruptcy, the law forces creditors to absolve the debts of the debtor, in order to give the debtor a fresh start and freedom. Absent bankruptcy it would probably be inevitable to bring back debtors prison and indentured servitude, which is a road to slavery. Moral bankruptcy operates along similar principles. Michel Foucault once hypothesized that there is an Internalized Other in each person's head whereby society conditions a person to cast society's judgment upon himself internally. To the extent that a person has a sense of social judgment, and an accounting of one's emotional capital, one acts in this capacity as bankruptcy court judge, and one then looks in the mirror and sees oneself as debtor to oneself as creditor, to the extent one failed in what one was morally obligated to give to oneself.

You were stupid in how you applied for a job, you did not try hard enough to obtain a goal, you did not put up enough of a fight to save a romance, etc. You look at yourself and declare that you are filing for moral bankruptcy. The judge then absolves all emotional debts, you are forgiven, you have absolved yourself for the sin against yourself that you had committed, and you move on with your life.

The definition of emotional maturity is explained by the theory of emotional capitalism. It is the constant forgiveness of small debts to other people in your life who have been good to you in the past. Someone annoys you with some small wrongdoing against you and you forgive them instead of seeking to recover what they now owe to you, and you forgive them in your emotions, and hold no urge nor feeling to get pain from them.

This is a sound way to do business in a capitalist economy. This is like a car dealer who pays off your loan as the cost of making the sale happen. Between two merchants who frequently do business with each other, forgiving small debts is a matter of convenience and practical necessity. Such is the definition of being emotionally mature.

In contrast, an emotional toddler is someone whose recovery of tiny debts owed to them is swift and extreme. Such people will throw a temper tantrum to make you feel bad if they feel bad and blame you in any small extent, either consciously or unconsciously. If they resent you, such as by categorizing you as the type of person from whom they blame their miserable lives, or if they feel that the type of person you are, or you specifically, have treated them unfairly, they will seek to recover what they feel owed in the most juvenile way possible.

Honor is defined as the quality of repaying and taking debts owed by you or to you according to your own internal moral ledger without needing any external pressure to be forced to do so. Honor and emotional maturity do not contradict, because an honorable man strives to repay outgoing debt (debts owed to others) whereas a mature man strives to forgive incoming debts (debts owed to him). Because you own debts owed to you, you may do as you please with them, and forgive them, and this is not theft. This is true if you owe a debt to yourself. In contrast you cannot force someone else to forgive a debt because that would be theft.

Debts can have orders of magnitude, also known as scale. A higher order debt can offset a lower order debt, for example, I owe you $50 and you owe me $5, we can cancel $5 by one debt paying off the other and now I owe you $45.

A kid may recover a lower order debt by being mean to them if the parent did something wrong, but the kid's higher order debt to the parent (being given life and love, etc.) outweighs it. The kid will not know it offset but the parent will, so the parent may think the kid wronged them and be mean to the kid to recover that lower order debt, which the kid may see as a new debt owed to them that the parent wronged them again. In this way, two people must calibrate their ledgers to each other or the result can be chaos if each feels owed debts which the other does not recognize or is unaware of.

Just as the absence of bankruptcy leads to slavery, the absence of moral bankruptcy leads to emotional slavery, whereby one person takes control of another person on account of real or perceived emotional debts so high they cannot be repaid. Such is evil and the antithesis of freedom, although one's honor may naturally seek to repay debts to the fullest extent one can.

An emotional thief is someone who seizes emotional capital without paying for it, either by intentionally failing to repay emotional debts earned in the normal course of business of social relationships, or by causing pain with no remorse, not giving what is owed on their side of the ledger. Such people are evil and have dishonor.

In addition to a ledger of what is owed to a person, we humans seem to keep a mental ledger of good and bad done to us today, what life owes us. If one person after the next after the next is mean to us, we reach and break our limit, and then throw a temper tantrum to be mean to random passersby to try to recover some of what life owes us. If life is very kind to us we feel blessed and elated to have a moral surplus, and may then be in a kind and generous mood towards strangers, repaying life for what it gave to us.

Interestingly, like men, nations and races maintain an emotional ledger, and may seek repayment of debts for wrongs or rights done 700 years ago or even older. This explains much about why war or peace exists.

Parenting is also informed. The unconditional love of a (good) parent for a child will forgive any sin in return for the joy of having a child. Also, maybe we try to protect children, not from a parental instinct, but because we feel they are too young to have done anything to deserve bad things happening to them. An emotional debt arises between two people from their actions and exists irrespective of whether one has "passed moral judgment" upon the other. Debts exist objectively, not subjectively, much as if someone loans you $20, your debt to them exists objectively because the $20 is a real physical object in your pocket. But it must be conceded that emotions and psychology are mental attributes, although what a person does is something which physically exists in objective reality, if only as what their voice says or what their body enacts (although in other books I have argued the mind and brain are identical, I don't intend to rely upon that premise in this book). What is owed and what one believes is owed may be identical, because only honor motivates most of the emotional economy, so only what people believe is owed will ever be paid, and a debt is not fully real unless we expect to collect on it somehow.

What is owed is based on the context of what you know. For example, if you know X, and because of X Jane owes you a debt, so Jane goes out of her way to be nice to you, and then you learn that X was never really true, then you now owe Jane a debt equal to what she paid you, or potentially greater if the ignorance was your own fault.

This has applications to Objectivism and Libertarianism. Objectivism is a cruel, strict master, which calls upon a person to be rational 24 hours a day, 7 days a week, with any intentional act of unreason deemed as black, putrid evil. Objectivism as ethics is to some extent a form of Perfectionism, and you are expected to be a smart person and achieve the very best that your ability could have made possible. That is a tough standard to maintain. Moral bankruptcy, if viewed as rational, can play an important role in an Objectivist's moral life.

In libertarian political philosophy, moral bankruptcy forms a basis for "real" bankruptcy, legal bankruptcy, absent which some might view it as a debtor immorally stealing what is owed to, and owned by, a creditor. Some libertarians view bankruptcy as theft. But it is a natural part of human existence. It also justifies the libertarian darling called jury nullification: if a jury knows there is guilt under the facts and the law, but feels the accused should rightfully be forgiven, then they may vote to acquit. The theory of emotional capitalism and moral bankruptcy can play an important role in the emotional health of Objectivists and libertarians, and everyone else, too.

GREED AND LUST: SINS, OR VIRTUES?

Let us begin with definitions and axioms, and then see where logical deduction leads.

Assume that a human being is an animal which speaks and thinks. The human as animal is body. The human as thinking entity is mind. The human as one who speaks is soul (personality, identity).

Let us assume that one human can be sexually attracted to another human because of one or more of three traits: body, mind and soul.

Define love of the body as animal love.

Define love of the soul as Platonic love.

Define love of the mind as Randian love.

We can immediately deduce that each of these three types of love possess fatal flaws. Animal love lowers oneself to a capacity one shares in common with animals and is not distinctly human. As such it lacks our highest capacity as humans. It is our basest and most disgusting nature. While the pleasure of the body is actualized, the mind and soul, our distinctly human nature and higher capacity, are ignored.

But Platonic love denies the existence of lust and the physical world. As such, it may engender mutual esteem, but not true love, since it creates regard but not sexual desire. Lust without love should not exist, but love without lust cannot exist. Platonic love shares all the faults of Plato: seek to deny the physical world, and you will repress and deny reality, and then reality itself will undermine you and condemn you to frustration.

Then there is Randian love. Ayn Rand lived this is her relationship with Nathanial Branden: she believed that one person's love of another person's mind, with no regard for liking the other person's personality and with no lust for them physically, that mere shared intellectual values and having in common a philosophy, could form the basis for love. Randian love leads to the repression of both body and soul: you love the mind, but do not like the personality and are not attracted to the body. Then your repressed desires will eventually explode, as when the Rand-Branden affair ended with fireworks.

A form of love exists which shares none of the above flaws, which we may term Aristotelian love. Aristotelian love calls upon each person to find a ratio of body to mind to soul which is the correct expression of what they want in a lover, and to then seek that. This can be expressed as a percentage. For example, a person may care 20% about body, 10% about mind, and 70% about soul. Or a person may care 60% about body, 15% about mind, and 25% about soul.

The aspect from Aristotle is the Golden Mean: you do not want to choose too much or too little, you want just the right amount, and your correct ratio is unique to you as an individual. Too much body and you are a mere animal. Too much soul and you are a mere ghost. Too much mind and you become a mere brain without genitals.

There may be feelings of guilt if one hews to an extreme and away from the Golden Mean, as, if, for example, one cares 96% about body, 2% about mind, and 2% soul. But this is a personal choice and it would be difficult to prove that you were objectively incorrect (or to prove that you are correct). What you desire is an expression of who you are, and the only wise guidelines are "know thyself" and "to thine own self be true."

Also, for love, what each person wants must match with what the other person has. If you care about soul and someone has a great personality and sense of humor and is friendly and loving, they might be perfect for you, but if what they love is mind and, let us say, you lack a college education and are coarse and unrefined, they will not want you. What someone is and what they want have no correlation: a person may have a great body yet desire a boyfriend with a great soul, or they may have a great body and crave only another great body for pleasure, or they may have a great body and care 33% about each if the three attributes.

In true love, if and when such a thing exists, you, what qualities you possess, will satisfy all or most of what your partner seeks and vice versa. And, in reality, there is an added even deeper level of complexity, because people often feel guilty about their desires or are confused by them and so will be dishonest and lie about what they really want, making it even harder to win a good match and find real love, since you will know if you love them but might find it hard to tell if you are what they truly desire. Something similar may be said of greed. Greed is the love of money, but it may be subcategorized into three types for analysis.

Getting money is the love of acquiring money, and is really the joy of spending money, of consuming value. We may call this selfish greed.

Making money is the joy one takes in the act of creating value, the pride that a maker has in the act of making something good, or the pride one takes in a job well done. We may call this proud greed.

Then, albeit more rarely, there is what may be termed economist's greed, which is the desire to plug into the economy and do one's job and perform one's role for the good of the economy, on account of the various economic theories which prove that it is a net benefit to society when the individual makes money. Economist's greed is honorable greed, the desire to do the work to pay all the other people in the economy who make the stuff you use, by making stuff for them to buy.

Selfish greed taken to an extreme will inspire one to theft or fraud or unethical behavior to maximize the amount of money one has. The rich people who engage exclusively in selfish greed may rightly be termed the evil rich, and there is no shortage of scams or government-enabled graft and corruption by the evil rich.

But proud greed to too great an extreme ignores the whole point of money, which is the joy of spending it and experiencing the pleasure it buys. Someone with too much proud greed might be a workaholic and work excessively, spending too much time making things instead of spending time with his family or enjoying a hobby, for example.

Economist's greed taken to an extreme can devolve into a belief, even among capitalists, that society is more important than the individual. A lot of actual economics professors are capitalists who believe this, but it undermines the moral foundation of capitalism, which is individualism. People may want to do their duty to society by working their job, but ignore their own legitimate needs for joy and pleasure. As with lust, in greed one should discover a ratio between selfish greed, proud greed, and economist's greed, by which one avoids being evil while still selfishly enjoying life. For example, one may be motivated 75% by selfish greed, 20% by proud greed, and 5% by economic greed. Or, if one really loves one's job, and does not enjoy shopping much, one may be motivated 50% by proud greed, 30% by selfish greed, and 20% by economic greed.

One final point on the topic of lust: if lust is not a sin, then being gay/lesbian/LGBT is not a sin, and every legitimate non-criminal sexual desire/fetish is not a sin, for the same reason. However things like pedophilia and bestiality are evil, because they defy human nature and the role and purpose of sexuality, which is sex and love with consenting adults. Children and animals lack human sexual capacity physically, so human nature could not have intended them subjects of sex.

This concludes my account of lust and greed as analyzed by analytical logic with special reference to Aristotle's ethical theory of the Golden Mean.

ENVY: KEEPING SCORE

Men can compare themselves to others and fall short in many ways. One can measure and compare:

Health,

Beauty,

Wealth,

Charisma,

Intelligence,

Luck,

Strength.

One can also compare accomplishments:

Family,

Friends,

Lovers,

Children,

Career,

Skills,

Education,

Amount of joy consumed,

Amount of money made,

Amount of joy your actions enabled other people to have the freedom to consume (social libertarian political activism), and

Amount of money your actions helped other people be free to make (economic libertarian political activism).

Because technically speaking a human should be good in every area, but in reality no one has the resources to pay the cost to achieve at a high level in literally every area, you will probably always envy at least one or more other people, if only because they chose to spend their time on an area where you spent far fewer resources and so in that area you achieved far less than they.

One might think then that wisdom lies in achieving the goals best suited to your personality and desires, for example, is your highest value becoming a doctor, or finding true love, or going on lots of vacations — because you have finite discreet limited "life resources" to spend (time and money being the big two) so you can't have everything. But in practice this wisdom can be difficult — you want to be a doctor with a love life who takes long vacations, and if you choose one you will envy everyone who chose the other two, intimately knowing the flaws of your choice but seeing only the virtues of theirs. A Buddhist might tell you to renounce the goal of achievement. A conservative, or a strict parent, might say you had better fucking achieve or else. Neither path will make the pain of failing to achieve hurt any less.

Wisdom dictates a different path: try your best to achieve but forgive yourself if you fail. Prioritize your goals and spend resources accordingly, mindful that, as Rand said, subjugating a lesser value to a greater one is not a sacrifice, but vice versa is (and see her essay on this topic, in The Virtue of Selfishness).

To paraphrase Nietzsche: esteeming the greatness of the achievements of other men enables us to hold the achievement of our own dreams a safe distance away from ourselves. He also might have said, or should have said: we are all of us human, all too human, and therefore must either move above our humanity or else forgive ourselves for being human. It is also instructive to study self-esteem, in light of Rand's The Fountainhead. Take sex, for example, with a focus on what is known as "body image problems." There are those who feel that if you are hot then you deserve to have sex and are worthy (really, that you deserve to be loved) and, if you are not hot, you don't. But being hot does not correlate with deserving to have sex, only, in a practical sense, for some people it has some small impact on the game of chance of getting lucky, and no more. Self-esteem is what correlates with deserving to have sex.

We can distinguish two things: a source of self-esteem, which can be attacked but can never truly be destroyed, and the pretense of self-esteem, which can be taken away. These two things can exist for any given purpose, for example, hotness is a pretense of self-esteem for the purpose of having sex, and can be taken away (if a man says "you look fat" to a woman or to a gay man, for example). But if, for example, the source of your self-esteem for dating is confidence, that cannot be destroyed, and a woman's rejecting you may test it but will not crumble it.

A body image problem arises if your pretense at self-esteem really is based on looks and you are plausibly critical of your own hotness. As Rand artistically rendered in The Fountainhead, pull out the foundation of self-esteem and the soul collapses: this is what Toohey does to Peter Keating, and what Dominique tries and fails to do to Roark.

One can have a source or pretense of self-esteem for any purpose: career, job skills, a hobby, a friendship, your religion, your favorite author or favorite music, any facet of your identity, and it can always be attacked or challenged by other people or events or even by new facts, but self-forgiveness is a very useful tool for repairing it or fortifying it. For example, forgive and accept your body and then fret no more over it.

The basic premise of being fat-shamed is that you owe it to other people to be perfect for them so if you're not then you don't deserve to be loved. In reality there is no objective rational reason why you would owe perfection to others or need it to achieve the relatively mundane social status of love and acceptance. You deserve to be loved, you deserve to have the boyfriend or girlfriend or wife or husband of your dreams, and you deserve to have sex at will. Every good human being does.

The only obstacle is that men can use low self-esteem to exploit and control women, which is also an LGBT problem as one gay man can do this to another, much as Toohey manipulates Keating because Keating's pretense of self-esteem as an architect arises from social approval (Toohey's art criticism as the voice of society), and so there are systemic structural elements in our social existence which enable attacks against our self-esteem at any time. Adults and "normal" people are less vulnerable — unless it is their sense of normalcy itself which gets attacked. While one is forgiving oneself for being less than perfect in a romantic context, it is also wise to forgive one's boyfriend or girlfriend or wife or husband for being less than perfect, although it is a personal decision how much is too much to forgive and when to walk away. Generally, flaws and faults should be forgiven, and such forgiveness and emotional maturity is necessary to have a healthy relationship, but pure evil should not be forgiven.

If confidence is a source of self-esteem whereas body image is not, and is a mere pretense, it may be asked how one achieves confidence. Roark in The Fountainhead is illustrative. He is a good architect, and he knows that he is a good architect. This is true even while at times in the novel everyone else is saying he is a bad architect.

You are a good person, and therefore you deserve to be loved, and your knowledge should always match the truth about objective reality, so you should know that you are a good person, and then you should know that you deserve to be loved, because these facts are true. You really are a good person, and you really do deserve to be loved. This in a sense is pride, and, in that sense, pride is a virtue, not a sin, and pride is the antidote to low self-esteem.

FORGIVENESS OF EVIL

We must ask: what if you commit a truly evil act? Is your own forgiveness enough? Or do you need God's? Or your victim's?

We must begin by asking: why did you do it? Did bad luck, circumstance, or a villain, drive you and pressure you to do it? Was it a necessary evil brought about by desperate times or an emergency? Where there is no freely chosen decision to act, there is no volitional free will so there can be no blameworthy nor culpable status.

But what if you commit the most evil sin? What if you fundamentally betray a friend, a family member, or, as I believe the most evil sin to be, what if you betray yourself and violate your integrity as an ethical human being?

What if you sell your soul, metaphorically, trading your moral righteousness and integrity to evil in return for what you want: money, power, sex, an easy way to gain success without doing hard work, or a sense of self esteem arising from how society sees you when you conform and betray who you really are by pretending to be someone else, or other vices like these? What if you looked the other way while your friend or your boss committed a crime? What if you fall into a life of crime yourself? What if you betray a friend and have an affair with his wife and lie to him repeatedly about it? Even worse crimes than these can also exist, especially in times of war or with political corruption. Even good men can be tempted to evil.

The great appeal of The Fountainhead (which nobody realizes) is that Ayn Rand addresses this. Peter Keating and Wynand both sin against Roark, but Wynand is forgiven. In the novel, climaxing at the end, Peter Keating sells his soul to Toohey for power and the pretense of self-esteem. Peter Keating gets his sense of self-esteem from how society views him, making him into the slave of social critic Ellsworth Toohey, who represents (and controls) the voice of society. Here I explore Keating's actual black sin of evil, betraying his friend and the voice of any trace of integrity left in his life, Roark, to Toohey, not even for any tangible profit but because Toohey has become his master and he has no self-respect left with which to resist the command of society for obedience.

Rand was cognizant of this betrayal as sin, and as Keating destroying his own soul, a long, drawn-out process which begins with his letting his mother pressure him to become an architect when he really wants to be an artist, grows when he abandoned the woman he loves to marry his boss's daughter to gain social status at work and in the eyes of the architecture professional, and culminates in handing evidence that Roark bombed Cortland Homes to Toohey, which Toohey wants to use to send Roark to jail, to break his spirit by force because no amount of social pressure or stigma has succeeded in getting Roark to contradict himself and renounce or sacrifice his soul to gain Toohey's (society's) favor. There is a point in the famous Toohey speech at the end of The Fountainhead where Toohey explicitly says that Keating sold his soul to him.

Rand even acknowledged this tongue in cheek where Toohey says to Peter Keating "ever read Faust?" (a German play where the main character Faust makes a deal with the devil Mephistopheles) when Keating hands him the contract that Keating and Roark signed for Roark to build Cortland Homes while Keating takes all the credit and praise for it, which Toohey needs as evidence in the courtroom trial against Roark, whereby Keating sells Roark to Toohey.

The scene much earlier in The Fountainhead where Toohey comments upon the Biblical verse "what should it profit a man, if he gaineth the world, but loseth his own soul?" (Mark 8:36), with Toohey replying "then to be truly rich one should collect souls?" is Rand's sense of humor about this issue of Keating selling his soul to the devil. In Ayn Rand's lectures on writing fiction she once said "nothing in my novels is accidental," so it is open season for us to read these religious interpretations into little details in The Fountainhead.

Wynand, too, betrays his own inner integrity, succumbs to pressure, and sells Roark to the masses to save his newspaper, at the end of the novel, again, for money, power, and the pretense of self-esteem that having built a newspaper empire makes his life meaningful. Toohey finds what Wynand built his self-esteem upon, the newspaper, takes control of it, and thereby breaks Wynand, much as he breaks Keating through his self-esteem depending on what other people think of his career and social status as an architect. This act, to betray your integrity in return for trivial sham rewards, is what I regard as the blackest sin.

But Roark forgives Wynand. Wynand in the end cannot forgive himself but as one final gesture lets Roark build the Wynand Building. He says to Roark, in the most poignant scene at the very end of the novel, "build it as a monument to that spirit which is yours . . . and could have been mine," which sums up the quest for integrity and speaks to his overwhelming sense of guilt for having betrayed Roark and for having betrayed and defiled the good in him (his friendship with Roark) in service to evil (his newspaper, the stupid masses who read it, and Toohey who controls them). But Roark forgives him and builds the building.

I think there are two lessons. If you commit the blackest sin, betraying your integrity, selling your soul to the devil, there is no external elements to this crime, it is merely your choice, so if you repent, and if you are a good person, you can forgive yourself. You control what is in you. Your moral status, whether you are good or evil, is within your control. Second, Keating simply is evil, and Wynand just is good, it is what they are, you are what you are and your choices and actions can't ever truly change your soul. If you are a good person, that will be with you always, and any crime to which you are driven, hands stained red with blood by ill fate, cannot change what you are. If there is still goodness in your soul, if you still see the light, if you know the difference between right and wrong, this is a sufficient basis to forgive yourself, spell out your sentence of penance for you to punish yourself, repent, pick yourself up and then move on. Were you truly evil you would know only the darkness, so if you can still see light, this is proof that you have a rational basis to deserve to forgive yourself.

This is if the person you betrayed is yourself. If instead you stabbed someone else in the back, if someone died for you to live, then, in moral capitalism, you owe it to the world to save someone, or to save as many people as whose lives you ruined. This explains why religions based on guilt are so often missionary religions. Even in this case, one can earn the repayment of debts owed. And wrapped around this entire analysis stands moral bankruptcy if you have the balls to absolve punishment for a sin as black as night. Even if you hurt others, the moral injury is a wound to your own soul, which you own, and thereby you own the debt and have the legal right to forgive it.

At no point in this exposition has it become apparent that you have any need for God or religion. Yours can be a Do It Yourself forgiveness of sins. You do not need God's forgiveness because your own forgiveness is what matters, and is the moral reflection of your soul, or your moral self-worth.

What if your crime has an external victim whom your actions have wronged? When you hurt someone, you sin against three beings: your own soul as your capacity to be good and the corresponding debt you owe to yourself to be the best you that you can be, your victim equal to the emotional capital (money and/or joy) which hurting them has robbed them of, and also you sin against society, the brotherhood of all men, our great human undertaking to build a world where we help each other to be as happy as possible.

The law exacts the payment of moral debts owed to

society (by fines or jail, the quintessential Nietzsche paradigm of causing pain to repay a debt from pain wrongfully caused), and this essay does not examine the laws as such, so I will not explore that area. You repay the debt to yourself and the debt to your victim with guilt, unless you forgive yourself, and unless you beg for and are granted forgiveness by your victim, in which you will no longer regard yourself as owing him your guilt. In a worst case scenario, if you are being crushed by guilt and depression, you can file for double moral bankruptcy: forgive yourself for your sin against your own soul, and forgive yourself for failure to obtain your victim's formal declaration of his forgiving you.

Ultimately if you repent with sincerity then there must still be good in you, which is a sufficient basis to "save your soul," pick up the pieces and try to put your life back together and be a good person from now on, and forgive yourself for having done evil. People's emotions tend to believe what other people say they owe, children especially so because they don't know any better and lack a frame of reference from which to doubt. Social capitalism relies upon external validation, and children and teens do so a lot, although adults do also, to a degree inverse to their emotional maturity.

Social capitalism is emotional capitalism as it relates to, and impacts, social interaction with your peers. Your moral ledger (your mental sense of debts and credits owed) guides how you behave towards others. How others treat you, and what they say to you, is external validation or contradiction, feedback which your emotions use to calibrate the accuracy of your ledger.

For someone who was abused or bullied, as a child or teen or as an adult, the bully is essentially telling you that you don't deserve to be happy, that you don't deserve to live, and your emotions will read that as external feedback. Your emotions can be tricked into thinking you have sinned and exact payment as guilt or self-inflicted punishment. Here the act of self-forgiveness will clear the emotional fraud off the ledger. You are not, and are never, to blame for being bullied or abused, because bullying and abuse are evil by nature and so will always reflect an unjust account of debts or credits owed.

Taken to an extreme, honor combined with guilt may lead to an act of suicide, because the person seeks to repay whatever debt they feel they owe by literally giving their life to their moral creditor, but this is irrationality, and filing for moral bankruptcy is always what such a person should do instead. At the point of death, one can no longer be good nor do good, so suicide arising from a moral basis of extreme guilt is a contradiction: one tries to do the right thing by destroying one's own moral capacity. Moreover no good creditor would ask that as repayment, so you should not ask that of yourself, and if others do then they are evil and their evilness toward you must offset whatever you think you owe them, and they can hold no moral claim upon you. Guilt can be crippling but here the wisdom of Rand and Nietzsche is that you must have the stoic discipline for your reason to control your emotions and reach into your soul and turn off the feelings that are not objectively warranted by what you really owe to yourself or to others in the long-term.

When someone dies, we pray that they will forgive us for what we did to them in life, and we also forgive them for whatever they owed us, because the relationship is over so it is time to close the ledger and reconcile all debts and credits. Usually we feel that we treated them unfairly and were too miserly and stingy and immature, which we know only when it is too late to correct, because we were greedy and were not forced to undertake an audit until now. If, after we reconcile the ledger, we find that we owe the dead a debt which we will now never be able to repay, then we hold and cherish our memory of them for the rest of our lives, to try to repay our debt. We feel sadness to pay to the dead what we owe them, by giving them our pain (our grief), and also as a signal to our friends and loved ones to request support and comfort in any amount that our friends owe to us or are willing to lend us.

HUMAN MOTIVATIONS

Some men give to charity to seek penance for the sin of greed, to atone for being rich. That is charity from shame. Others give to charity out of an overflowing abundance of joy, that they are so happy and prosperous that they want everyone else to share their joy too. While the result is identical from the point of view of the recipient, shame is evil, and joy is good.

Our reaction to perfection is similar. Some of us, if we see someone with a perfect body or a perfect personality, immediately feel that they deserve to be loved, which reminds us that we ourselves are less than perfect, and then we feel we don't deserve love, and are sad. In times like these we must instantly forgive ourselves for being less than perfect and move on.

Other types of people, seeing someone who seems perfect, will simply feel glad for them, and share in their happiness, because they have self-esteem and confidence, and the perfection of others does not challenge and call into question their own worth. That is the type of person who can give to charity because they are so happy and proud that their joy overflows and spills over to give to others.

The perfection of others as a challenge to our own sense of self-worth relates to a similar syndrome in all social interaction: the fear of rejection. If we "bare our soul" to someone else, if we assert not merely a minor detail about ourselves but something essential to our identity, of if we seek to share something personal and deep and meaningful with someone, we expose ourselves to rejection and make ourselves vulnerable. If you are to do so, you must be prepared to instantly forgive yourself for not having been good enough for the other person in the event that they criticize or attack your self-esteem.

Two types of people can face opportunities for rejection with other people without fear: those who are so confident that they don't expect to be rejected, and those who know that if they were rejected they would forgive themselves immediately and completely for it, and know how to do so.

Obviously it goes without saying that you owe it to yourself to act for the sake of the best within you and to thereby actualize your highest potential for joy and happiness. To actualize your highest potential is to act for the sake of the best within you. In Objectivism (from a certain point of view) your soul, your highest potential, and the best within you, are the same thing. To be good, and to be happy, you must live life to the fullest with no regrets — or with regrets that you can find it within yourself to forgive yourself for. Failure to do so is the ultimate sin, for which you will need your own forgiveness, if at the end of the day you want to be able to look in the mirror.

POLITICAL MOTIVATIONS

The inflicting of pain in order to obtain payment for an owed debt may be referred to as retribution, justice, or revenge. Such is the motive of many voters and political activists. For example, someone sees a forest get destroyed, then becomes an environmental activist to get revenge against polluters on behalf of the trees. Or someone is denied an employee benefit by her boss and then votes for a pro-labor leftist politician to get revenge against big business. Or a man sees a picture of an aborted fetus and becomes a pro-life activist to get revenge equal to the loss suffered by the fetus which he feels is now a debt owed by the pro-choice movement that created the freedom for it to happen.

But in politics, as in social reality, there can be an equivalent of emotional maturity, which in this context we might name policy maturity. A higher order debt cancels out a lower order debt by offsetting the amount owed. Just having a job at all may be so important to long-term survival that the employee owes more to the employer for creating the job than the amount lost on a denial of requested benefits. Big business, by making the money that enables a society to be prosperous, might pay for conservation efforts which otherwise the human race could not afford — after all, dirty energy is cheap and clean energy is expensive, so if we couldn't afford to pay for it we would burn more coal and oil. The debt a fetus owes to its mother for existing probably exceeds any debt the mother would owe to the fetus as an obligation to be pregnant with it and give birth to it, or, at the very least, the debt of fetus to mother equals what mother owes fetus so the two debts would offset and leave a net zero.

Generally, emotional irrational thinking among voters is the equivalent of being an emotional toddler in social reality while logical rational thinking and seeing the big picture enables policy maturity. One final point is that misattribution and misdirection may be present as well: you feel that one individual injured you and owes you an unpaid debt so you seek retribution by voting for a politician who will punish the group or category of people to whom your debtor belongs — a race, by voting for a racist politician, for example. This is obviously irrational and insane, because other people are not morally responsible for what one person has done so you should not punish a race for a debt owed by an individual. But in politics many voters behave irrationally and lack maturity.

Men give their votes to social justice crusade politicians to pay wronged groups of people for what you feel you as a member of society owe to them, so that the government will pay off your moral debt for you. You may also vote for a particular politician if you feel that he personally helped you, either individually or by aiding a group or class you belong to, because you owe a moral debt to them. And then there are voters who feel blessed to live in a good society and feel it is a repayment of what one owes for being given this blessing to vote for a politician who will fight for goodness and virtue and truth and justice. Libertarian policy is generally superior to socialism, but such a basis for votes in emotional capitalism are usually based on how you feel about the politician, not how you feel emotionally about his policy. There are many ways in which forgiveness and sin play out in politics. People see a group or class of citizens whom they feel have been wronged, and then vote for a government to right that wrong, to give those people what they are owed, which is called fairness and justice and is really the repayment of debts owed so that both sides of the ledger even out. But the libertarian point of view is that, if you feel a wrong has been done, it is your job, not the government's job, to help fix it, spending your own money, not other people's money, because you have the right to spend money you own but lack the right to take money from others even for a good cause.

But what if by yourself you don't have enough money to fix it, so collectively pooling money is necessary for justice? Then persuade large numbers of others to freely and voluntarily donate to your charity, don't force them to give money against their will by government tax and spend. The money you would owe to the taxpayers you robbed would equal any justice of debt repaid to an oppressed class.

It is not the job of government to forgive us for being human and for making mistakes, by removing our freedom to make mistakes and replacing it with a dictator's control. Instead, forgive yourself by doing the work necessary to get what you want, and then you will obtain it, and the only thing that could stop you then is bad luck, for which you should feel no blame. I am not a Christian but believe strongly in this: "Ask and ye shall be given, Seek and ye shall find, Knock and the door shall open." (Matthew 7:7). If you want money, go get it. If you want a job, find one. If you don't choose to get what you want, that is a sin, but government can't fix that, that is something only you can do. If you hit rock bottom, are poor or homeless, file for moral bankruptcy, stop feeling sorry for yourself and start over.

There are also those who feel they are not worthy to be happy and lack self-esteem and feel they don't deserve to live, so embrace any dictatorship that will punish them to give them what they feel they are morally owed: suffering, a total lack of responsibility for making the decisions which control your own fate, and, eventually, death. These people need to forgive themselves and seek a sense of self-worth, but, absent that, we the living must not allow ourselves to be dragged into Hell by those who are half dead already.

When the government has total control, regardless of whether politicians are good or evil, the citizens have no free will, hence cannot make mistakes, hence can do nothing for which they need to be forgiven. But it is also true that, lacking free will, they can commit no blessings nor virtues and do nothing that is right and good, having no ability to make any decision or ethical choice of right or wrong at all. Such a scenario is manifestly repugnant to the moral lives of human beings.

With respect to politics, it is also wise to remember this Bible verse: "All those who sin are a slave of sin." (John 8:34). If you sacrifice your moral integrity, you will very quickly find yourself under the control of evil men, and, ultimately, of evil politicians or dictators. The evil in you will seek out the evil in them, and, having turned to the darkness, you will not have the light within you to shine at them to drive them away. If someone else controls your self-esteem then they can destroy you, so your soul becomes their slave. Although I am a Libertarian, I want to point out that any type of politician may seek to exploit you: the socialists, liberals, conservatives, and, if there were any, libertarians. Remember with warning what Toohey says: "It's the soul, Peter, the soul, not whips or swords or fire or guns. ... The soul, Peter, is that which can't be ruled. It must be broken. ... You won't need a whip — he'll bring it to you and ask to be whipped."

MORAL ECONOMICS

Let me point out that, in Atlas Shrugged, in the scene where James Taggart accuses Cherryl of having a shopkeeper's morality and she accuses him of seeking the unearned in spirit, Rand gets at her closest to articulating an idea that pervades Atlas Shrugged, the idea that moral value and economic value is equivalent, that morality and finance are comparable. Esteem is to be paid for by being a good person, success is to be paid for by doing the right thing ethically. Moral value as a human is to be earned by doing the hard work of living an ethical life. And you earn your social and romantic relationships by doing the work to make the relationship work and to give the other person what they enjoy in return for you getting what makes you happy.

Emotions are like money, in this way: money is a loan, in that the owner of a $1 bill is owed $1 worth of value; the dollar bill is a promissory note that the economy is to give back $1 worth of value if the owner hands over the dollar bill to the economy. An emotion is a record of money on your moral ledger; for example, if you love someone, then you owe them your devotion because they have already paid you for it by being the person you are in love with or by loving you. Your emotions tell you what you owe and are owed, just as a $10 bill tells the economy that it owes you $10 worth of value, $10 worth of goods and services to consume, because you lent the economy an hour of labor at your job that paid you a salary of $10/hour.

Values — moral values — can be earned, stolen, bought, sold, traded, and, yes, loaned or borrowed or repaid. The thesis of this paper is to take this concept seriously, and then understand how bankruptcy works in a moral economic system. Much as the finance system and capitalism in the USA could not function absent bankruptcy law to govern debtors and creditors in the event of insolvency, so too moral capitalism cannot exist absent a formalized system of forgiveness. It is then a logical analysis of human nature to say that our emotions evolved as our ledger in moral capitalism, telling our conscious minds to take what we are owed and give back where we owe debts.

Feelings and emotions, in this way, are vital to ethics, and it is also worth noting that emotions are not inherently irrational and illogical as such, and play an important role in a rational life. However your subconscious mind may have a different belief about your debts than your conscious mind, which is where reason and emotions might conflict, and you must reconcile how you feel with what you believe. Do not assume that your reason is correct and your emotions incorrect, nor vice versa, but undertake a substantial detailed analysis to discover the truth.

It might be asked why the human brain tends to subconsciously dish out pain (or pleasure, as discussed in the next chapter) to repay moral debts and credits. My position is that this is simply a feature of human evolution, although one might see it as a moral fact, that your brain tries to give you what you deserve. Humans seem to have evolved from primates who survived as pack or tribe animals. They formed tribes, and families within those tribes, which would have required a precise calibration of how to assign help to each other, as for sharing food, or hunting, etc., and who owed what to whom. Our biological ancestors were "social animals," to take a phrase from Aristotle which is probably better translated as "social by nature." As such, not only our reason and mind, but also our social reactions, are highly evolved. I see moral economics as an aspect of the human brain arising from our evolution as social animals.

Here I will share a happy thought. So you sinned. You let yourself down. You failed. Your wife and kids are mad at you. You're not the greatest person at your job. You wanted to do something very much but lacked the courage or the will to do it. You reasoned that you should pursue a path but let irrational fears talk you out of it. Or something similar. You sinned against your own soul by failing to act for the sake of the best within you. Or you sinned against someone else. You didn't buy the best gift for your girlfriend because you didn't want to spend the money. You were not supportive of a friend in a time of need because it was too difficult and stressful. You were a doctor and made the wrong decision and a patient died, or you were a soldier in a war and one of the other soldiers died in combat to rescue you and you survived but they died.

You feel guilt, to make yourself suffer in order to repay the debt that you cannot otherwise repay: a debt you owe to yourself, or to someone else. For the doctor who owes life to the dead or the soldier with survivor's guilt, in their emotional capitalism ledger they may feel the need to hurt themselves with guilt in an amount equal to the value of life itself, because they feel they owe a life to the person who died.

But that's humanity. That's being human. You sinned. So what else is new? We all fail. Everyone does. Forgive yourself. Use moral bankruptcy. You are a good, special, wonderful person. You still deserve to be happy. Repeat that: you deserve to be happy.

You're a good person and you deserve to be happy. And you deserve to love, and you deserve to be loved. Never forget that. They say "forgive and forget." Yes, forgive. But never forget that you deserve to be happy.

CONCLUSION

This essay has succeeded in explaining a theory of emotions, motivations, and ethics, which explained everything that it set out to explain. Guilt and shame and anger have been explained by reference to the infliction of emotional pain to repay, or retake, pain as payment for moral debts that are owed. Honor was explained as the willingness to repay the moral debts that you owe to others without being forced to do so, while emotional maturity was explained as a tendency towards forgiveness of small debts on a daily basis. Moral bankruptcy was presented as the paradigm for self-forgiveness, using finance and economics as a metaphor for moral economics.

However, happiness, love, sadness and fear have not yet been discussed. Just as the human brain inflicts pain upon someone in order to be repaid for a moral debt that they owe, so, too, the human brain evolved to feel pleasure as payment for moral credits that are owed to it. So your brain rewards you for being a good person, to self or others, with happiness, literally, with emotional pleasure, because you earned it. Happiness is the pleasure that you give to yourself when you owe yourself a moral credit, while love is the pleasure that you give to others when you owe them a moral credit for them having been a good person or having been good to you (precisely, for them having been or done something worthy of your love). If this is true, then living an ethical, moral life is the key to living a happy life.

In this way, happiness, which is pleasure given to yourself for a moral credit, is the opposite of guilt, which is pain inflicted upon yourself for a moral debt, and love, which is pleasure given to others for a credit, is the opposite of anger, which is pain inflicted upon others because of an unpaid debt. Happiness and love can be termed the positive emotions, while guilt, shame and anger are the negative emotions.

I am tempted to define another emotion, pride, and say that pride is the opposite of shame, in the sense that pride is the pleasure you feel from people seeing what a good person you are, that you reward yourself with for having impressed others with your virtue, while shame is the pain you feel when others watch you fail. However, I am resisting this temptation, because the word "pride" has many meanings, some positive and some negative: pride can mean joy in being good, or one's own knowledge and conviction that one is a good person, or joy in other people seeing oneself as good, or pleasure as reward for having done a good job, but it can also mean hubris and arrogance, or an unjustified inflated ego.

It is even true that, from the Objectivist point of view, self-knowledge of one's own virtue is the key to self-esteem, whereas virtue in the eyes and opinions of other people is a mere pretense of self-esteem (usually), so it is very ambiguous whether pride is actually virtuous or unethical, and the definition of the word is too muddy to admit of clear and precise usage. Pride, as an emotion, would merely be a type of happiness, happiness arising for a specific reason, anyway.

With respect to the seven major emotions: happiness, sadness, love, fear, guilt, shame, and anger, this leaves only fear and sadness in need of an accounting. I briefly touched upon sadness before, when discussing grief and mourning, but I will elaborate more broadly here. Sadness seems to be a biological reaction to the experience of things going wrong in your life, such as when you start crying or feel tired and apathetic, and it seems to have evolved to trigger a person to act to remove the cause of the sadness, or, at least, to notify one's friends and family so that they will try to help you.

On this analysis, sadness is similar to guilt, except that guilt is a specific reflection of you having done moral wrong, whereas sadness is precisely a reaction to things in your life going wrong, regardless of moral blameworthiness. To the extent that your guilt makes you sad, this is the emotional expression of the moral fact that having done the morally wrong thing will cause things to go wrong in your life.

The author views fear as largely a biological mechanism that evolved to make an animal flee from and run away from a threat. The only extent to which fear now matters for humans from a psychological or ethical point of view, as opposed to a biological point of view, is when the threats are social or emotional or moral, rather than a danger to survival, in which case the brain feels fear or anxiety to motivate escape.

Fear can be perfectly moral and rational if you are in a situation where running away would really be the right thing to do, such as if you have to flee from a fight you know you would lose in order to save your life, but fear can become irrational or unethical if the situation is such that you feel a need, or a desire, to escape, but the right thing to do in this situation is to face your fear, which really means, to stand up and put up a fight against whatever is threatening you.

For example, being in a new social situation where you have no friends can be scary, and might trigger social anxiety, and then you must choose whether to stay and try to talk to people and make new friends, or whether to leave because you can't stand your anxiety. The fear is your desire to flee, but what you really fear is the shame you will feel if people reject you. As such, fear itself can pose a moral test, as to whether you face your fear, or flee from it in cowardice, and this is the most common scenario where fear will possess any moral significance, as seperate and distinct from a mere biological urge to run away from physical life-threatening danger. A similar case is the person who fears starting a new job or a new career, or an athlete who fears a clutch moment in a sports game, because they fear failure, and what they truly fear is the guilt they will suffer if they fail, or the shame they will feel if other people watch them fail.

This is why, if you are practiced at the art of filing for moral bankruptcy, and you can use self-forgiveness to eliminate guilt, shame, and anger, this will also eliminate your fear of failure or your fear of rejection, because what you really fear is the guilt or shame that you will inflict upon yourself if you fail, and, with moral bankruptcy, you will no longer have to live in fear of those other negative emotions, and so you can have the ability to act, and to go after your life goals, be they friends, family, career, money, love, or whatever, without fear of feeling the pain of guilt or shame if you fail, and without fear of anger. In this way, the theory of moral bankruptcy can help you to succeed and achieve in life.

TO BE LOVED, LOVE; TO BE LIKED, BE NICE TO PEOPLE; TO BE AN ADULT, FORGIVE PEOPLE: EMOTIONS AND SOCIAL INTERACTIONS, EXPLAINED

INTRO

This book explains a system for improving social skills and psychological health and emotional well-being. This system is based on a set of principles, based on math and logic and reason. Each principle is stated in a clear, simple way. Each principle is then given an analysis. Math and logic are used for this analysis, but only at a level that every person can understand.

The math and logic describes basic aspects of human existence that you will relate to. You will see what I mean when you read the book. This book is, basically, the math and logic of depth psychology, and how it can help you master your emotions, make people like you, and live a happy life.

The book assigns a separate chapter to each principle. As a result, this book has a lot of chapters, but each chapter is short and easy to read.

This is a self-help book. But it is not typical. It is unique. It uses math and logic to explain the depth psychology behind a variety of social dynamics in human behavior. If you understand how these dynamics work, you can use that understanding to your advantage, to further your goals.

This is not a book of words of affirmation. There are other books that say "You are a good person, you deserve to be loved, you deserve to be happy, you are special, you can achieve any goal you set your mind to." I have written other books that say exactly that. Such statements are all true. But this book doesn't say that. Instead, this book will tell you, in detail, *how* to get people to love you, *how* to be happy, and *how* to achieve your goals. With precise, specific details. With tactics, and strategies, that you can understand.

This book's unique purpose is not give you warm, fuzzy feelings in broad, general terms. Many other self-help books, my own included, already do that. Instead, this book tells you strategy and tactics for maximizing your social skills and social interactions, and explains the psychological and social dynamics of the groups of people you interact with, at work, at school, in business, in friendship, socially, or romantically. With tips for how to handle each social dynamic, described using math and logic.

A lot of this book is focused on common mistakes and pitfalls that people fall into often, and intelligent, clever ways to avoid those pitfalls, or ways to climb out after you have accidentally fallen in. Ways to escape from anger, addiction, depression, and fear are described. Tools for motivation are offered. But this isn't just about problems and bad stuff. It is also about being happy, friendly, cheerful, trusting, faithful, positive, and optimistic. How to be more polite. How to get people to like you. And ways to become more emotionally mature and insightful and perceptive about other people's feelings.

If, after reading this book, you go out into the world, and you feel like you now understand more of the different types of behaviors you are seeing people do, than what you knew before reading this book, then, for this book, it is mission: accomplished.

I hope you enjoy reading this book as much as I enjoyed writing it for you!

THE BASICS

The basic element of the analysis is a mathematical logical equation, of the form, for example:

Y +N to O as Emotion for O +N to Y as Speech.

So let's go through each item of syntax (symbols) one by one and explain the semantics (what it means).

Y: You. The Self. A representation of the person from whose point of view the analysis is conducted.

+: Positive, giving, giving something from the person on the left side of the equation (Y) to the person on the right side (O). + indicates giving a benefit, or something positive. The contrasting symbol would be –, which indicates a detriment, or something negative. + is plus. – is minus.

N: A number. Indicates a quantifiable, measured amount. It can represent any amount, until you plug an actual number or unit into the variable N.

To: indicates that the +N was given "to" O (from Y).

O: The Other. A representation of another person, who is not Y, but whom Y interacts with.

As: This indicates that the next term will qualify the form in which the +N manifested.

Emotion: Indicates that the +N was a positive emotion.

For: For the benefit of. The expression "A for B" means that A was done because of B, A exists because of B, B pays for A, A repays B, or A is for the benefit of B. The expression on the left was payment "for," or given in return "for," the expression on the right.

Speech: A qualifier of the +N that O gave to Y, that it was spoken verbal speech or written words, in some form of language.

So, here, Y gave +N as emotion to O in return for O giving +N to Y as speech. So this statement could mean, if we plug those variables in, if N is a small amount, it be translated to mean that O was polite towards Y, so now Y likes O.

But, if N is a large amount, it could mean that O asked Y to marry them, so Y is happy and loves O.

The statement can mean different things based on what values we enter into the variables in the expression. That is why this system is flexible and can describe most any social situation, as we shall see.

MORAL DEBTS

Let's consider three typical Hollywood movie scenes.

In an action movie, the villain kills the hero's friend, and then the hero tells the villain: "You will pay for what you did to my friend!" (This is a version of a quote from the movie Hellboy 2, where the hero kills the villain's accomplice, and the villain says to the hero "You will pay for what you did to my friend," to which the hero sarcastically replies: "You take checks?")

In a drama, a man is released from prison after serving a twenty year sentence, and an onlooker observes: "He paid his debt to society. He earned his freedom." (Many movies have scenes like this.)

In a police thriller, the older veteran cop saves the rookie cop's life from a shooter, and then the veteran says to the rookie: "You owe me, kid. You owe me one, big time." (A ton of cop drama TV shows and action movies have scenes like this.)

Please carefully consider the above quotes. They speak of debt. But they do not mean a literal money financial debt. The villain isn't going to pay the hero with dollar bills. The debt to society was repaid with jail time, not by the criminal defendant giving a sum of money back to society as compensation for his committing a crime. The rookie cop does not owe a precise dollar sum to the veteran, as repayment, and the veteran does not expect money from the rookie cop. That is not what they mean when they say these things.

What these quotes mean is a moral debt. To be repaid by pain.

The hero will make the villain repay the moral debt he owes, by inflicting emotional pain upon him, equal to the pain caused by his friend's death.

The criminal paid the moral debt that he owed to society, by means of the pain he suffered from two decades in jail, with the understanding that the pain of twenty years in prison is pain equal to whatever wrongfulness or pain his crime caused to his victims for which he was convicted and sent to prison.

The rookie cop owes a moral credit to the veteran cop, who now owns a moral credit against him, to be repaid by the rookie doing or saying something of benefit to the veteran, equal in amount to the good that the veteran did to the rookie.

This book takes the position that moral debt and moral credits, to be repaid by the infliction of emotional pain or the causation of emotional pleasure, permeates human existence, and affects every aspect and facet of human life, but it does so mostly subconsciously, by means of emotions, so most people are still not consciously aware of how it works. So everyone gets what those movie quotes mean, but no one realizes that financial debt is a metaphor for moral debt, that this is central to human existence, and that most human morality is a system of repayment of what is owed and earned. This book will explain how it works, and what it means, to repay a moral debt through emotional pain, or to be owed a moral credit that has earned emotional pleasure. This book will analyze emotions, using that insight.

Of course, the first objection that will enter everyone's thoughts, is that this idea would mean that most human emotions are a mere this-for-that buy-sell trade, a trade of pain for debt, or pleasure for credit, which would suck all the joy and meaning out of the depth and beauty of real human emotions, and which would be limited in usefulness as a tool for analysis. Other sections of this book address, and refute, that objection. I will fully explain my theory first, and then refute objections and challenges to it, later.

O –N to Y as O wrongs Y, O does wrong to Y.

This statement implies that O now owes a moral debt to Y in an amount equal to N.

Then there exists a set of possible solutions:

Y –N to O as to right a wrong: this can be called Justice, Retribution, or Revenge.

If done by laws and government, often by imposing jail time onto O as –N, it is called justice. If done by one private individual against another individual, it is often called revenge, or vigilante justice.

Or: O +N to Y for O –N to Y, O pays penance or pays compensation to Y or apologizes to Y for O's wrongdoing.

Or: O –N to O for O –N to Y: O feels guilt to atone for doing wrong.

Or, as discussed elsewhere in this book: Y F(–N) = Zero, Y gives spontaneous, complete forgiveness to O. Then O does not owe a moral debt to Y after having been completely forgiven. Such forgiveness is a gift, instead of a trade of –N for –N (revenge) or +N for –N (compensation).

Definitions:

Time T: The time when a statement happens.

= Now: A qualifier of T, that means today, the present.

= Future: An alternative qualifier of T, which means some time in the future.

= Past: Another T, which means at some point in the past.

The statement

O +N to Y at Time T = Now

implies that Y owes a moral debt to O at Time T = Future where the amount of the moral debt is equal to N, which can be repaid to O by Y as

Y +N to O

Or (maybe) as

Y –N to Y for O.

So we can state this as:

(Y +N to O or Y –N to Y for O) for (O +N to Y)

Take this statement:

Y +N to Y as Action for Y +N to Y as Emotion.

We can also write this statement as:

SD MD(N) owed to SC for SC MC(N) owed to SD.

Let's define the terms:

SD: Self as Debtor. When you loan emotional capital to yourself, you owe yourself a debt. One person, but in relation to themselves as debtor (to themselves as creditor, on the other side of the expression). SD receives a moral credit as a loan and thereby owes a moral debt.

MD: Moral Debt

N: A number. Any quantifiable measured amount.

Owed to: Indicates that SD owes MD(N) to SC. SD owes a moral debt to SC in an amount equal to N.

SC: Self as Creditor. Gives loans of moral credit in return for moral debt, and receives repayment for moral debt.

Loaned to: Indicates SC loaned N to SD. SC's credit to SD

equals SD's debt to SC.

This statement can also be stated as:

SD +N to SC at Time T=Future for SC +N to SD at Time T=Now.

At: Means the expression on the left happened or took place at the time value on the right.

What does this mean? The expression is broad and could describe many things. Its precise meaning depends upon the values that fill the variables. It could be that you loaned an amount of courage to yourself necessary for you to ask your boss at work for a salary raise or a promotion, which moral credit you repaid to yourself by actually asking your boss for a raise or promotion. It could be that you loaned yourself the self-confidence and trust to ask someone out on a date, which you repay to yourself by doing so, the happiness and satisfaction that comes from it.

Why does this matter?

This book has a theory of the emotions: guilt, shame, anger. That they arise because the human brain naturally seeks to inflict emotional pain to repay moral debts. For anger, if a person owes you +N, and they don't repay with +N to Y, you exact payment by causing them pain equal to –N to O. For shame and guilt, a person naturally repays +N to Y with +N to O, but, where Y is unable to, the human brain evolved such that, naturally, Y will try to repay unpaid +N to O with –N to Y. Shame is pain repaid for a moral debt to others or to society. Guilt is pain inflicted upon the self to repay an unpaid debt that self owes to self.

Anger: Y –N to O as Anger (to cause pain) for O –N to Y as perceived moral wrong O did to Y.

Shame: Y –N to Y as Shame (pain) for Y –N to O as social mistake or awkwardness or social failure for Y owed +N to O (behavior that you owe to society, or benefit that you owed to someone else).

Guilt: Y –N to Y as Guilt (pain) for Y –N to Y as unpaid moral debt for Y +N to Y.

This book will show that anger, guilt, and shame, are factors in a lot of social scenarios and social dynamics. The book shows how to use forgiveness to master your emotions and take control of these situations. This takes the form:

Y F(–N) = Zero (to Y and/or to O).

This book describes forgiveness, by metaphor and analogy, as "moral bankruptcy," that you wipe the moral debt off the emotional ledger, you forgive the debt, and absolve the debtor. If you do that, then the self, or the other, doesn't owe you anything. And if no one is owed pain, then the human brain has no natural urge to inflict such pain. Then you can eliminate the guilt, shame, or anger, not by repressing it or hiding it, but by forgiving the underlying emotional unpaid debt that was causing it when the brain tried to inflict pain to repay or take repayment for unpaid moral and emotional debts.

Moral debts: what you owe

Moral credits: what you are owed

In general, moral debts are repaid with the infliction of emotional pain, while moral credits are paid off with the providing of emotional pleasure.

O +N to Y as Love (pleasure) for Y +N to O as Love and

Emotional Support (a moral credit that Y was owed by O)

Y +N to O for O +N to Y. For example, as Speech, Y is polite to O because O was polite to Y.

Y –N to Y for O, for O +N to Y. Y owes a moral debt to O but cannot repay, so Y feels Guilt (Y causes emotional pain to Y on behalf of O, to repay O by giving Y's pain to O).

Y –N to O as Anger for O –N to Y as Action (as Moral Wrongdoing that Wrongs Y). O owes a moral debt to Y for having morally wronged Y, so Y takes payment as Anger, by getting angry at O, and thereby causing emotional pain to O to repay the moral debt that O owes to Y.

They're moral debts and moral credits, not literal financial debt of loans and amounts of money owed. I have to say this over and over again, and repeat it, so that people understand. I'm not talking about money debts. I'm talking about moral debts. That you owe it to people to be good to them. And that when someone morally wrongs you, they thereby owe you a moral debt. Or that when you do good and do the right thing, you are owed a moral credit by the people you did good for (self, or others). It's moral debt. It's moral bankruptcy. It's not money debts. It's not actual bankruptcy.

I am talking about morality. Please wake up and pay attention. Please understand.

DEFINITIONS: +N, −N

To: at, directed at, towards.

For: Because of the morality and moral debts or moral credits of, for the benefit of.

+: Plus.

−: Minus.

N: An amount, a quantity.

As: Manifested as, embodied as, taking the form of.

$: Physical.

+N: Positive energy
Being there, showing up, staying, not leaving
Emotional support
Love
Happiness
Pleasure
Kindness

Hope

Trust

Compassion

Politeness

Respect

Friendliness/Being Friendly

Cheerfulness/Good Cheer

Optimism

Commitment

Honesty/Openness

Emotional availability

Doing work to make a relationship work

Appreciation

Being supportive in the face of negativity

Staying positive

Giving them a loan of social or emotional capital

–N: Negative energy

Not showing up/Leaving early

Rejecting someone

Keeping someone waiting/Sending someone away

Pain

Anger

Sorrow

Misery

Distrust

Pessimism

Gloom

Hopelessness

Depression

Sadness

Guilt

Shame

Rudeness

Disrespect

Theft of emotional capital

Negativity

Being annoying

Being manipulative

Being insecure (to lack trust)

Being emotionally dysfunctional

Being abusive

+$N:

Logistical support

Money

Tangible achievement

Tangible favors

Being relied upon

Doing work

Making stuff

Physical love

−$N:

Theft of money

Dishonesty

Being unreliable

Being manipulative

Using someone as a means to an end

Taking stuff

Physical violence

Y: The Self, You.

O: The Other, another person.

P: To perceive, to believe, to know. X P(Y) means that person X perceives Y to be true or believes that Y is true or holds Y as knowledge.

Hide: To repress, submerge, or misdirect one's emotions. X Hide(Y) means that X is hiding Y.

F: Forgiveness, to Forgive, moral bankruptcy.

G: A Goal, any goal, any end state that is the object of desire.

Day: Today's good luck or bad luck, and anyone who happens to be near you today.

Life: The sum total of everything that has happened to you, either –N or +N.

EMOTION AS MORAL DEBT AS A FORM OF MEMORY OF PRESENT EXPENSE TO BE REPAID BY FUTURE ACTION

An explanation of the eight most important human emotions:

Memory as moral debt or moral credit in emotional accounting ledger.

For example:

Y –N to O as Anger for O –N to Y as Action at Time T = Now

Y –N to O as Action for Y –N to O as Anger at Time T = Future

This theory explains eight of the most important emotions in human existence:

The negative emotions: (pain for moral debts)

(1) Anger: Y –N to O as Pain (for O –N to Y as Action, usually)

Solution: Forgive. F(–N) to O = Zero Anger.

(2) Guilt: Y –N to Y as Pain (for Y –N to Y as Action, usually)

Solution: Forgive. F(–N) to Y = Zero Guilt.

(3) Shame: Y –N to Y as Pain (for Y –N to O, usually)

Solution: Forgive. F(–N) to Y for O = Zero Shame.

(4) Sadness: Y –N to Y as Pain for Life –N to Y as Action (usually, but can also be Life –N to Y as Pain)

Solution: O +N to Y as Family and Friends' Support and Comfort. That is the best solution.

(5) Fear: Y Avoids Risk N = Risk of –N to Y (and, sometimes, Y –N to Y as Pain/Sadness for Y avoided Goal G for Fear of Risk N = Attempt G –N to Y and thereby Y caused Y to miss opportunity G out of Fear)

Solution: Confidence that you will forgive all –N against yourself if you fail. That eliminates, for example, fear of rejection, fear of guilt or shame as fear of failure, and fear of disappointment. Then give yourself a loan of courage and self-confidence that you give to yourself as Y +N to Y where +N = Risk(–N).

The positive emotions: (pleasure for moral credits)

(6) Love: Y +N to O as Pleasure (for O +N to Y, usually)

(7) Happiness: Y +N to Y as Pleasure (for Y +N to Y as Action, usually)

(8) Pride: Y +N to Y as Pleasure for Y +N to O as Action or as Accomplishment of Goal G (usually)

Emotions as pain inflicted to repay a moral debt owed by a moral debtor or pleasure given to pay off a moral credit owed to a moral creditor. Emotions are not irrational. Emotions are logical and mathematical and exist for a reason.

Conceding the theory of negative emotions as the infliction of emotional pain to repay moral debt, we can then see the extreme usefulness of a theory of forgiveness as moral bankruptcy, where Y F (–N) = Zero N owed to Y. This serves to prevent emotional accounting from becoming excessively mean and cruel or potentially unjust and too harsh to survive. Moral bankruptcy sets the debtor free, and gives them a fresh start in moral reality, set free from pain imposed upon them.

An emotional decision is one based on seeking to obtain positive N for oneself (or others), or to inflict negative N upon others (or upon self), in contrast to a rational decision, which seeks the best means to achieve a Goal regardless of the emotional pain or pleasure that those means causes to others or to self. However, often, emotions, and managing emotions, is itself a part of the most rational means to achieve a Goal, at least where human action is involved.

F: FORGIVENESS

The mathematical logical formula for forgiveness:

F(–N) = Zero: When you forgive negativity equal to N, the result is zero, a moral blank slate, no emotional negativity.

Y F(–N) = Zero to O: Where Y had felt an emotion equal to –N towards O, Y has forgiven O for an amount equal to N, such that –N becomes Zero.

WORDS

Saying these words to someone is Y +N to O as Speech where N = Amount of politeness and amount of being pleasant and nice. Obviously you can't say these in a mechanical or formulaic or robotic way, or as though you were reading a script. They have to flow naturally. And you have to really mean them. But these are some examples of +N as Speech:

The seven ways to say something nice to someone and to make someone feel good about themselves because they talked to you:

I. Salutations and Farewells (Y +N to O as Politeness)

Hello

Goodbye

II. Words of Polite Request (Y +N to O as Politeness for Y –N to O as Asking O to Do Something for Y)

Please

Please (do this)

Yes, please.

Thank you

You're welcome

III. Words of Sympathy (Y +N to O for Life –N to O)

How are you?

I'm good. How are you?

How's it going?

Hey, what's up?

I'm glad that you are feeling well/I'm glad that (something good).

I'm sorry that you are feeling bad/I'm sorry that (something bad happened).

I'm sorry that you feel that way/I'm sorry for you that (something bad).

Best wishes.

My condolences.

Get well.

Feel better.

I hope (person) gets better/feels better.

Have a good day!

Have a nice day!

IV. Words of Affirmation (Y +N to O for O +N to O)

I'm happy to see you!

You look nice today/Those are really nice (clothes they are wearing, your hair looks really nice/you have a really nice haircut today, your makeup looks nice, that's a really nice sweater, etc.).

(Any compliment.)

V. Words of Thankfulness or Words of Apology (Y Offers

Y –N to Y for O)

Thanks, I appreciate that/I appreciate your help/I appreciate you saying that.

I'm sorry. I apologize.

I'm happy to help (you).

It was no problem.

I hope you enjoy (thing)/I hope you have a good time doing (event)/at (place)!

I understand. That's okay.

VI. Words of Joy or Words of Love

I like you!

I love you.

Hey, do you have any plans for/are you doing anything on (this weekend/tonight/lunch/dinner)? Would you like to hang out with me? Maybe doing (event/hobby/activity) with me?

(Smile at someone.)

(Listen to a person who is talking to you. Listen actively. Listen intently.)

(Laugh at someone's joke.)

VII. Words of Respect

I value your opinion

I appreciate you telling me that/I appreciate your honesty

Thanks for telling me that. I learned something from you today.

I agree.

I'm glad you said that, I found that helpful, I learned a lot from what you just said.

(Address someone by name. Their first name if in a casual setting. A formal Mr./Ms./Mx. And their last name if in a formal setting.)

GIVE THEM A LOAN

Emotional capital/An emotional loan: Giving someone a loan of emotional capital means giving them love, hope, trust, and treating them like they are a great friend or treating them like they are the love of your life, now, today, early in the relationship, before you know whether they are a good person or a bad person and whether they will treat you well or badly. They then repay the loan by being a good person and loving you and having a good relationship with you over the lifetime of the relationship. First you love them, then they earn your love.

In its most extreme form, this is love at first sight. In a more moderate form, it is becoming best friends with a person you just met. In its most minor form, this is, for example, going to a party, and giving a stranger a small loan by saying hello to them and talking to them warmly and opening up a conversation with them, which loan they repay by having a polite friendly conversation with you for a few minutes. You take a risk, you invest, you give a loan, then the other person is nice or friendly or loving to you for a period of time, and that is your profit on the loan.

People are rational moral actors trying to maximize their self-interest. To get people to be nice to you, you have to give them something in return. So if you are nice to them, they will be nice back to you in return, because you were nice to them. That is what "giving a loan" means. You are nice to them, before you know for sure whether they will be nice or nasty back to you in return.

In contrast, you take a loss if the other person does not repay the loan: if they leave, if they are mean, if they mistreat you and are rude and disrespectful to you and treat you badly. You can take an emotional loss on the loan if what you get is less than what you gave, or you can try to recover the value of the unpaid debt from the other person by causing them pain equal to your moral loss as what they owed you, by breaking up with them, un-friending them, coldly walking away from them at the party and not talking to them anymore, etc.

You have to give people loans of emotional and social capital, to take risks, in order to "make a profit" socially and emotionally, you have to take the risk of investing in your friends and your romantic relationships, to make them grow, or else you won't have any. A loan is a risk. And, to be emotionally mature, you must forgive small loans that go bad in your life, with the people in your life and with the people whom you love, and to forgive, constantly, daily, instantly and completely.

Things to which you can give a loan:

A person

Self (for example, loaning yourself self-confidence)

Others

A lover (for example, loaning them your trust)

A friend (loaning them the time and energy to hang out and have fun with them)

A romantic partner (loaning to them the belief that they are destined to be the love of your life, and treating them as such, before you even know everything about them, loving them before you know whether they deserve your love)

A situation (for example, a loan of courage and conviction to take a risk to move to an apartment in a new city or move to another country)

A new job or career (for example, loaning it hope, loaning to it the grit to overcome early anxiety and fear about it, and loaning it the time it takes for it to develop to see whether you like it and/or are good at it)

A new belief or theory or idea (loaning it the resources of an experiment to test it and see if it works for you, and then loaning it the resources to put it to work for you in real life)

A religion or philosophy

An activity or hobby or interest (for example, loaning it your time and energy, and expecting some enjoyment as repayment from it after the work is done)

An undertaking or venture or goal-seeking endeavor or quest (for example, loaning it the belief that achieving that goal will make you happy, to give a sense of meaning and purpose to your quest)

ON FAITH

O seeks to achieve Goal G

O requires positive energy (self-confidence) = N in order to achieve Goal G

Y +N to O as faith, trust, hope, believing in O that O can do this

O +N to Y as achieving Goal G in order to repay Y for Y's trust and confidence in O.

That is the psychology of why, if Y expects O to succeed, O is more likely to succeed (or, if Y expects O to fail, O will more likely fail). Your faith in them is what morally motivates them to succeed.

When you are a member of a team, if every team member needs to excel in order for the team to win, then it is imperative that each team member trust the other members of their team and believe in them and have confidence in them and have faith in them, because the team will lose if they don't. The best way to unlock each team member's maximum +N is by the other team members' +N to them.

It doesn't matter whether your faith in them is justified at the outset. They will earn it, over time, by performing. You don't have to know that someone will succeed in order to have faith in them. You don't know. You don't know in advance whether they will succeed, or fail, but you choose to have faith in them that they will succeed, anyway. That is why it is called faith, or trust, or hope, that you give to them, or loan to them, as opposed to merely a prediction that they will win.

In contrast:

Y –N to O as distrust or doubt

Then O's +N + Y's –N = Less +N for O, less self-confidence and courage and conviction with which to achieve G, which makes O less likely and less able to achieve Goal G.

The principle is similar if it is Y who believes in Y as self-confidence and believing in yourself.

Y +N to Y for G at Time T = Now as a loan

Y achieves Goal G by means of self-confidence = N at Time T = Future

Y repays loan of Y +N to Y at Time T = Past with Y +N to Y as joy and happiness for success of Goal G at Time T = Far Future.

This is why, if a person has hope, then they still have the chance to succeed, but if they lose their hope, then they have no chance to succeed: it is because, if they still have hope, they can rationally justify giving themselves a loan to pay the emotional and moral costs of continuing the fight, as Y +N to Y for Goal G, and then they continue to give themselves loan after loan of hope and self-confidence and courage until they win (or lose), thereby still being able to win, but, if they lose hope, then they can no longer (rationally) give themselves a loan, because it would be a guaranteed loss, with no return on investment and no interest or principal repaid, so they lose all "emotional financing," the emotional and moral capital with which to continue the struggle.

I think that when the Christians say that they have faith in God and that they believe in God, what they really mean is precisely the opposite: that they want God to have faith in them and they want God to believe in them. God would have no use for their faith, and God would not need their faith. In contrast, they would very much need God to have faith in them. And the so-called "Protestant work ethic" simply means that, if God shows faith in you, and you are given the opportunity to succeed, then you should earn God's faith in you by succeeding, by doing the hard work and labor and time and effort to succeed, thereby proving that you were worthy of God's faith in you.

This theology contrasts sharply with Kierkegaard's "Stairway to Heaven" critique, that some Christians believe, which says that humans are always so weak and sinful that we could never earn God's faith, and so we must always ask for it as an undeserved gift, arbitrarily given for no reason.

MAKING OTHER PEOPLE LIKE YOU BY BEING NICE TO THEM

Other people liking you: O +N to Y.

The key to getting other people to like you is:

Y +N to O (as Speech, Action, Emotion, Loan of Emotional Capital, Loan of Social Capital (trust, hope, love)).

O +N to Y for Y +N to O.

And resist the temptation to:

Y –N to O (being mean to them, if you want them to like you or if you like them),

or Y –N to Y for O (being mean to yourself, self-deprecating, self-insulting to yourself, on behalf of someone else, to get them to like you. Being negative towards yourself is a type of being negative, which no one likes and no one enjoys).

O +N to Y for Y +N to O

It isn't a direct this-for-that buy-sell trade. It's a bit more complicated than that.

Y +N to O at Time T = A long period of time

Eventually, O likes Y (If O can like Y, if O ever will like Y, if O + Y is a combo of types of people that will get along and like each other)

Then O +N to Y Because O likes Y.

If Y's strategy is "O +N to Y for Y +N to O," then "it's not about you," instead "it's about them." The focus of Y should be on +N to O, which is what Y controls, Y should not be focusing on O's +N to Y. Y should not be selfish or have an ego about it, in the bad sense of those words, instead Y should focus on sincerely liking O and projecting positive energy +N to O. Y's +N must be real and sincere and Y should mean it, it can't be fake and phony. If it's fake, it's like trying to buy something with counterfeit money, which is fraud, whereas the right way to earn value is by paying for it with real legitimate hard-earned cash. Money is a metaphor for this, but it is literal truth that Y is trying to earn O's esteem by +N to O. To be loved by someone, you must love someone. To be loved, love.

HOW NOT TO BE MANIPULATED, AND HOW TO HANDLE CONFRONTATION

Adult/Mature: Y +N to O for O +N to Y.

Childish/Abusive: O –N to Y as Threat of Higher O –N to Y If Not Y +N to O.

O uses –N if O lacks the social skills to use +N or if O is simply too mean, not nice, or too evil to use +N.

Can be O Threatens O –N to O for Y If Not Y +N to O.

O threatens –N to O because of Y unless Y agrees to give +N to O.

For examples:

–N: "Go on a date with me or I'll cut myself."

+N: "I really like you a lot. Please go on a date with me."

–N is the abusive, dysfunctional, passive-aggressive, personality disorder way to interact with people.

+N is the healthy, mature, sane, good behavior, normal way to interact with people.

For another example, of a married couple with kids who are having a fight:

–N: "I will take the kids away from you and take them

with me to another country and you will never see your children again if you divorce me."

+N: "Please, let's see a marriage counselor. I want to stay in this marriage, I love you. But, if we can't work things out, let's at least stay civil and polite, and stay friends, for the sake of the kids."

Definitions:

Exceed: Is Greater Than. That, if N Exceeds N(2), the amount equal to N was higher, greater, a bigger number, than the amount equal to N(2).

N(2): A second N in a formula, not the same number as N. N, by implication, means N(1).

So what does Y do after O Threatens Y? Y has to confront O, and have a confrontation with O.

How does Y do that?

There are two paths. By means of +N, or by means of –N.

Healthy, adult, mature confrontation:

Y +N to Y for Y Confront O where Y +N to Y Exceeds O –N to Y. And then Y +N to O when Y faces O in confrontation.

For example: Y gives Y a loan of emotional capital as hope and trust and self-faith and self-confidence in Y that Y can handle this (and/or Y seeks emotional support for this from Y's supportive friends and family), then Y confronts O, Y engages O and talks to O, Y tries to get help for O and to be nice and friendly to O and to talk O out of it; if that fails, Y takes legal steps to protect Y, O (and kids) from O.

Y says No to O (assuming, in these examples, that Y doesn't want the date, or that Y wants the divorce), but Y says it in a polite way, and it is spoken in a nice, respectful way, evidencing respect for O, so that Y's No = Y No to O as Y +N to O. This way, O does not perceive Y's No as equal to Y –N to O, for which O would then counter in anger with O –N to Y. If Y's No is perceived as +N to O by O, then that is Y +N to O, which negates O's feeling of O –N to Y for Y –N to O, which would leave O feeling Zero towards Y, and that ends the confrontation.

Abusive, juvenile, immature confrontation:

Y –N to O for O –N to Y, where Y's Goal is for Y's –N to O to Exceed O's –N to Y.

Example: Y gets nasty and abusive back to O and Y Threatens O, with Y's goal being to be more mean to O than O was to Y, and for Y's threats to be worse and more scary, to threaten and bully O into backing down from O's threats.

Later this book will discuss the difference between positive confrontation and negative confrontation:

In positive confrontation, the strategy is Y +N to Y as Emotion and as Action, and Y +N to O as Action, and the goal is for your +N to Exceed your opponent's –N. That your positive energy, your maturity, your responsibility, and your good cheer and love, overcame their negativity.

In negative confrontation, the strategy is Y –N to O as Emotion, Speech, and Action, and the goal is to use your –N to Exceed the enemy's –N. This very quicky becomes a race to the bottom where the worst person wins. That is not a good way to win. It is neither nice nor smart.

It becomes a war of bullying.

If O wins, then Y changes Y's No to Yes out of fear and intimidation. Y says Yes, when Y doesn't want to, and Y really means No, because Y fears O's Threats. This, then, only lead Y to repress Y's true feelings, which was a No, until Y explodes in anger. And then O will create a bullying dynamic against Y, to force Y to stay. This leads to a dysfunctional, abusive relationship.

But this tends to only happen if Y tried to use –N to counter O's –N. If Y instead chooses the strategy of +N, Y can gain the confidence and self-trust to leave the relationship, to exit, to leave O, by means of Y giving a loan of emotional capital equal to +N to Y, where N equals the emotions of self-confidence and self-trust and self-faith that are necessary for Y to confront O and/or to leave O.

Or, if Y wins, it is because Y was so mean and nasty and scary to O that Y pressured and scared O into abandoning O's initial threats. But then O's Threats made Y become a mean, nasty, scary, angry person. That is not a good, healthy way to win the confrontation. And the relationship between O and Y would continue to be defined by the dynamic of –N. Hence be abusive and dysfunctional. Even if Y doesn't date O or if Y divorces O, and Y scared O into not acting on O's threats if Y does so.

"Give yourself a loan" of self-confidence and self-trust and self-faith (having faith in yourself) that you are able to succeed. To enable you to face confrontation.

How do you give yourself a loan?

It's easy.

You spend it (use it) today.

You pay for it (earn it) in the future.

It's not complicated.

And, using the term "loan" for this type of thing is a metaphor. I use finance and capital as a metaphor for emotional capital and social capital. Emotional capital is love, trust, faith, hope, optimism, positive energy, good vibes, everything you have to loan someone (or to yourself) at the start of a relationship or to undertake a goal, in order to have the confidence and the trust and faith to do it. Social capital is what you spend (really, what you do) to make people like you and to become part of a group or be in a relationship.

Loans are a metaphor. An analogy. I'm not talking about literally giving people actual loans with real money. Wake up.

Pay attention. This is a metaphor only.

But then that leads to another useful metaphor. Moral bankruptcy. As the forgiveness of loans of emotional/social capital. As the forgiveness of debt. It's a useful way to understand how to forgive self and others. For the guilt/shame/anger that you may feel you owe to them.

The reason why people who have hope will put up a fight, is that they can rationally justify giving themselves a loan. If you have no hope, then you can't give yourself a loan, at which point the fight ends.

Manipulation:

O Threatens –N to Y unless Y gives Goal G to O

O's –N to Y Exceeds Y's –N to O

What can Y do?

Y more –N to O until Y –N to O Exceeds O –N to Y: Confrontation, fight, make it be more trouble than it is worth.

Or:

Y seeks help from X: The law and police, friends, a third party, a person in a position of authority, and X –N to O where X –N to O Exceeds (O –N to Y and O –N to X)

Of, if Y is stick in that situation and cannot fight back:

Y Ignore (–N) = Zero, until Y exits, Y leaves or escapes from O and from that situation.

Y should never give G to O unless Y is forced to. If Y gives G to O, usually O –N to Y anyway, and Y has signaled weakness to a bully, and then O asks Y to give a second goal G2 with threat of –N, and then O asks for G3, and then G4, and then GN where N equals the number of iterations of this cycle. If Y allows O to bully Y, it won't end, unless and until Y causes it to end.

HOW TO SAY NO TO SOMEONE

O asks Y for a Yes

Y wants to say No to O

Y No to O = Y –N to O

Y is afraid that O will get angry at Y if Y says No

If Y says it politely and/or with apology, it becomes

(Y +N to O as Y –N to Y) for (Y –N to O as Y saying No to O)

Then Y +N to O = Y –N to O

Then O does not owe any –N to Y as Anger, Y has offset the moral wrong (of hurt feelings) to O so Y owes no moral debt to O

O might still get angry, but this anger is unjustified because of Y's politeness and/or apology, and so Y can safely ignore it without guilt.

COPING WITH REJECTION

If Y asks O to be their friend, or to be their work-friend, or to date them, or to be their lover, if O rejects Y, or Y thinks that O doesn't like Y, if Y takes it personally:

Y P(O −N to Y) where N = Value of Y.

That Y feels a wrong or a negative directed at Y where the amount is equal to the very value of Y themselves, that N equals the value of Y as a person, the value of Y's life, because Y as a person is what was rejected by O, that O didn't like Y as a person enough to accept Y. Or, if O's acceptance would have been joy = +N, then O's rejection equals the same amount of negative where sorrow and sadness = −N and N sadness = N joy that would have been.

The solution is:

Either:

Don't take it personally, don't perceive rejection as O −N to Y.

P(rejection = Zero).

Or:

If you take it personally, and it hurts: Forgive yourself for having failed and for having been rejected.

Y F(O −N to Y) = Zero.

Give yourself a fresh start and an emotional blank slate. Use moral bankruptcy. Then try again, without owing any fear or guilt to yourself for your next attempt because you failed the last time.

HOW TO HEAL

"Time heals all wounds." "Forgive and forget."

Definitions:

P: Perceive (to perceive, to think, to remember, to be aware).

For example: Y P(O +N to Y) means Y perceives O +N to Y, or Y thinks that O +N to Y is true.

Forgetting about someone who has hurt you is the most insulting thing you can do them. It is worse than anger. Worse than hatred. Worse than making a plan to murder someone. It is the worst insult. That they, and what they did to you, doesn't matter to you enough for you to think about it or remember it.

But

If Y Forget O

Then

Y P(O –N to Y) = Zero and (Y –N to O for O –N to Y) = Zero, Because Y Not P(O Anything). Y P(O = Zero).

Then Y P(–N to Y from O = Zero).

So, if Y forgets about the hurt that O gave them, then Y is unaware of any pain, Y feels no anger towards O, but also Y knows no self-disadvantage from having been hurt, because Y has forgotten about it.

To forget, or to forgive, is not the same thing as to repress, or to hide. Each of these four things is exactly what it is.

To forget means to forget.

To forgive means to forgive.

To repress means to repress.

To hide means to hide.

This discussion involves only to forget.

TO FORGIVE ANGER

Y –N to O as Emotion for O –N to Y as Action.

Then Y –N to O as Action for Y –N to O as Emotion.

So Emotion –N = Debt of –N that Y owed –N to O as Action.

This is the paradigm of petty, vindictive anger directed as people around you to recover what you are owed for perceived wrongs against you.

Debt = Future based on Now, or Now based on Past.

Emotions hold memories of what is owed. Emotion is memory of morality, and of moral debts (and credits), to be later repaid as inflicted emotional pain for debts, as anger to others or guilt and shame to self, (or given as emotional pleasure for credits, as love to others or happiness to self).

The solution to solve petty, vindictive anger: Is forgiveness.

Y F(–N) = Zero owed to O.

Moral bankruptcy. Y forgives the debt owed to O. Y absolves debtor O of debt –N owed to O instead of giving the – N debt owed to O as anger. Then the emotion of anger ends, because the anger was just the memory that stored the debt on your emotional ledger, and the debt no longer exists, it was wiped away by moral bankruptcy.

The paradigm of forgiveness, as emotional maturity. To forgive, instead of anger.

Anger, as a biological responsive, is hardwired into the human brain. If something, or someone, annoys us or anger us, we get angry. It is natural.

Forgiveness is not easy. But it is virtue. And it can be used as the foundation of a system for emotional health and psychological well-being.

ON MORAL BANKRUPTCY

How to use moral bankruptcy to fight guilt, shame, anger, fear of rejection, fear of failure, fear of shame (social anxiety).

Y in Social Situation with O

Y –N to O by accident as goof/awkwardness/mistake

Y –N to Y for O as Guilt, Shame

Maybe also: Y –N to O as Anger for Y –N to Y as O –N to Y (Anger because of Guilt)

Y –N to Y as Fear of Guilt, Shame, Anger, as Denying Y a Loan for Future Social Attempts (Fear of Failure, Fear of Rejection)

Solution:

Y F(–N) = Zero. Y forgives Y. Y forgives O for judging Y in Y's perception of O and for Y's anger at O for causing Y's guilt.

Then Y gets a fresh start.

Then O +N to Y for Y +N to O as social success,

Or:

If failure again, then forgive again, and repeat until success.

EMOTIONAL MATURITY

What is the difference between an emotional toddler and an emotional adult?

If Y is an emotional toddler, and O –N to Y, then immediately Y –N back to O, as Action, frequently as being rude or getting angry at O or throwing a temper tantrum.

But, if Y is an emotional adult:

Y (as an emotional adult) is the master of Y's emotions, so, whenever someone is rude to Y or annoys Y or if Y thinks that they don't like Y, when O –N to Y, as Emotion, Speech, or Action, Y stops, and thinks, and decides how Y wants to react to that –N directed at Y:

Do I retaliate with anger? In emotion? In speech? In action?

Do I forgive?

Do I forget and ignore?

Do I hide and repress, until some time in the future?

Y may still choose to do Y –N to O for O –N to Y. But the emotional adult thinks about it first. The child doesn't think first. For the child, –N to others is an instinctive, automatic, instant reaction to any –N directed to them. So they have no self-control.

That's the difference between maturity and childishness.

PASSIVE-AGGRESSIVE BEHAVIOR AND REPRESSION

Definitions:

Hide: A Hide from X (B), means A hides or is hiding the action, emotion, or whatever, that is equal to B, from person X. A might be aware of A's Hiding either consciously or subconsciously, and A might be aware of B either consciously or else only subconsciously.

Passive-aggressive behavior: Y Hide from O (Y –N to O)

For example, talking trash about someone else behind their back, to vent your anger at them. For example, you are angry at someone for a long time but lack the ability or desire to express your anger directly to their face.

There are three possible solutions:

(1) Honesty: Get angry to O to their face, say mean things to them, vent, and let that cleanse the –N out of your system,

(2) Forgive, Y F(–N) = Zero, or

(3) Continue passive-aggressive behavior indefinitely. But then it will cycle until N builds up to the point where Y no longer has the ability or will to hide an N of that size, then Y explodes in anger to O's face as –N.

Repression: Y Hide from Y (Y –N to Y as Guilt or Y –N to

O as Anger or some other emotion or feeling or belief, such as Fear of desire for Goal G = –N, or Fear of attempt to achieve Goal G = –N). For example, Y secretly desires to make the attempt to achieve Goal G, but Y's fear holds Y back, so Y has chosen not to make the attempt for G, and now Y is repressing his/her/their desire for G, in order to make the decision not to seek G more tolerable.

There are three possible solutions:

(1) Honesty: Recognize how you really feel and come to terms with it and accept it and express it openly. Get angry at Y or O to their face, vent, express your honest emotions and feelings, and let that cleanse the –N out of your system, or, in the desire example, realize that what you really want to do is to go after Goal G, and you cannot eliminate your desire for it, so go for it, choose to go after Goal G despite your fears, and with courage and bravery to yourself as a loan of self-confidence = Y +N to Y for Goal G.

(2) Forgive, Y F(–N) = Zero, for example choose not to seek Goal G and then forgive all guilt, shame, and regret for that choice, and totally commit to it, and eliminate all –N that you had been repressing, or

(3) Continue self-repression behavior indefinitely. But then it will cycle until N builds up to the point where Y no longer has the ability or will to hide an N of that size, then Y explodes in anger (or guilt, or whatever) to Y's face as a total nervous breakdown or to O's face as –N as a fight and anger or confrontation or argument.

You can't hide from your feelings forever. The truth always comes out in the end. This can have either embarrassing and humiliating results, or even life-threatening and self-destructive results, sometimes.

Forgiveness is the best solution, but honesty is second best. To intentionally continue passive-aggressive or self-repressive behavior is wrong.

Misdirection is another type of passive-aggressive behavior, where O –N to Y, but either Y is too cowardly to –N to O or Y is too weak and O too powerful for Y –N to O, so Y assigns blame for O to a scapegoat, and then Y –N to scapegoat for O –N to Y. The choice to assign blame in this case is entirely subjective and irrational, but it is deemed Y +N to Y for Y –N to scapegoat, and Y Hides it from Y. Y can also scapegoat someone else for Y –N to Y and then Y –N to O to offload Y's guilt onto their scapegoat, or Y can scapegoat the Self for the benefit of an Other. The question, then, is always, if someone is angry at you, are they really angry at you, or are they angry for some other reason and they are misdirecting their anger towards you, and, if so, what do you do about it? It is irrational so there is not much you can do.

HOW TO ALWAYS BE CHEERFUL

How to be a happy, cheerful, positive person:

Forgive F(–N to Y) = Zero

O/Day/Life –N to Y
Y F(–N) = Zero
Y +N to O/Day/Life

For example:

Life –N to Y: Some terrible tragic accident. Someone in your family is diagnosed with a severe illness. You trip and break your leg. And then your health insurance declines the bill for medical treatment for your broken leg.

Day –N to Y: You're having a bad day today, you get bad luck, you miss the bus, there is a hair in your morning coffee, your favorite chair has gone missing and you have to sit on a very uncomfy chair. So you're in a bad mood, which means you have a tendency to get angry at anyone around you, to punish them for the bad luck that today gave to you.

O –N to Y: Person O was rude to you. Person O dumped some of their anxiety and fear onto you as –N. Person O said or did something that hurt your feelings. Person O vented their own annoyance by means of them saying or doing something negative towards you.

Then:

F (–N) = Zero: You forgive. You file for moral bankruptcy, on behalf of yourself and what anyone else owes to you. The moral debt that Life, or the Day, or person O, is forgiven, the debt absolved, taken off the books, wiped out from your moral ledger. You are owed no +N and you owe no one any –N.

Day –N to Y, Y F (–N) = Zero owed to Day, is the very definition of "emotional maturity," that a true adult is someone who forgives all of the minor annoyances of the day, instead of getting angry about those annoyances, and so is calm and rational and happy. Contrast the "emotional toddler," who is grumpy and resentful and tends to get angry at everyone nearby, which they do in order to try to reclaim revenge for all the wrongs done to them, in a juvenile, immature, hurtful way.

Then:

Y +N to O: Y is nice to O. Not forced being nice or faking being nice. Y is nice to O, and really means it. No anger, resentment, or malice. Just love, kindness, and respect.

Y +N to Day: Y is nice to everyone who happens to be near them.

Y +N to Life: Y projects positive energy and good cheer and optimism and happiness about life in general. Friendly, cheerful, positive. Everyone likes this type of person. You will be happy to be this type of person.

And, of course, the person who hurt you might be yourself. Then:

Y –N to Y

Y F(–N) = Zero

Y +N to Y as Self-Love.

REMEDIAL ACTION

If you make a mistake socially or do a social faux pas, as Y –N to O, these are some things you can do:

Make a self-deprecating joke about what you did as Y –N to Y for Y –N to O. It doesn't have to be all that funny. It's the thought (the moral intention) that counts.

Apologize, as Y –N to Y offered to O for Y –N to O. Don't make it dramatic. Just say enough so they know you are sorry.

Affirm the other person, be very nice to them or say something nice about them and flatter them, as Y +N to O for Y –N to O. Make sure they understand you are making the effort to be nice to make up for it. +N as an implied apology for –N.

These are constructive behavior solutions.

In contrast, shame, or guilt, or anger because of shame, are destructive coping behaviors.

THE DOWNWARD SPIRAL PATTERN: INTRO TO THE DOWNWARD SPIRAL

Pattern:

Y –N to Y as Action for Y –N to Y as Emotion for Y –N to Y as Action for Y –N to Y as Emotion, to infinity until Sum(–N)=Point of Explosion.

For example, the drugs and/or alcohol downward spiral to drug addiction or alcoholism. You feel sad, so you drink or do drugs. Then you feel sad because you drank or did drugs. So you use more drugs and/or alcohol because you feel bad and trashy because you used drugs and/or alcohol. That would, in theory, just spiral, until you were doing so much drugs and/or alcohol that your life was in danger.

Solution: F(–N) = Zero breaks the cycle. So you would forgive yourself for the last time you used, and then not use the next time (at least, not because of your prior usage).

SELF-ESTEEM

Here I introduce another set of definitions:

SE: Self-Esteem

+SE: Positive self-esteem, or an amount by which your self-esteem goes up.

–SE: Negative self-esteem, or the amount by which your self-esteem goes lower.

SE = What +N or –N Y feels that Y deserves, in sum.

+SE = Deserves +N to Y.

–SE = Deserves/are owed –N to Y.

SELF-ESTEEM AND DEATH SPIRALS

Definitions:

SE: Self-Esteem

+SE: High Self-Esteem, or an amount by which SE increases

–SE: Low Self-Esteem, or an amount by which SE declines

SE = the +N or –N that you expect to receive and that you feel you deserve.

Y +SE for +N to Y.

+N to Y affirms Y's +SE.

Y –SE for –N to Y.

–N to Y affirms Y's –SE.

Y –SE for O –N to Y as Abuse or for Y –N to Y as Self-Abuse.

Y +SE for O +N to Y as Being Nice and/or Loving or for Y +N to Y as Self-Love.

Because SE = Expected +N/–N, if Y has +SE, Y will seek out, demand, and expect, +N from O, and will surround themselves with Others who will give +N to Y.

So O +N to Y will cause +SE, but +SE will cause Y to seek out O who will give +N to Y. So +SE becomes a self-fulfilling prophesy upward spiral.

If Y has –SE, Y expects O –N to Y. So Y will gravitate towards Others who will Abuse Y. Then it becomes a self-fulfilling prophesy downward spiral: Y –SE because O –N to Y, and O –N to Y because Y chooses those O because Y –SE.

This can be described in math as:

Y –SE.

Y Seek Out (O –N to Y) Because Y –SE.

O –N to Y.

Y –SE for O –N to Y.

Solution to the death spiral formula: Y +N to Y, be nice to yourself and treat yourself with respect, until you recover enough self-esteem to put people in your life who will love and respect you and affirm a higher self-esteem. Also Y F(O –N to Y) = Zero for Y, Forgive yourself for the pain and shame and low-self-esteem inflicted upon you by the abuse of others.

The spiral pattern can exist in several forms:

The Fight:

X –N to A as Anger for A –N to X, plus

A –N to X as Anger for X –N to A

Then cycle repeatedly, and with each cycle, N increases, until:

Fight, confrontation, explosion, or

Forgiveness of –N by X for A and/or A for X = Zero, or F(–

N) equals a de-escalation in the amount of –N as perceived moral wrongdoing against the Self that was forgiven. For one person to forgive the other person, is for the forgiver to "be the bigger adult," to be the grown-up in the relationship, in comparison to an emotionally immature person, who doubles down on their anger, to get what they perceive is the revenge and justice they are owed, by getting angry at the other person for wrongs committed against them, in order to cause pain to the other person equal to the pain that the other person caused to them.

The Downward Spiral of alcoholism and drug addiction:

Y –N to Y as drugs and alcohol for Y –N to Y as Guilt and Low Self-Esteem

Y –N as Guilt and Low Self-Esteem for Y –N to Y as drugs and alcohol (and drugs-and-alcohol-induced behavior)

Cycle, and N increases with each cycle, until:

Death or a total nervous breakdown, or

F(–N) = Zero, as forgiveness of the guilt that comes from being an alcoholic or a drug addict and the moral failure that is perceived to be, and

Y +N to Y, where +N offsets –N, as Recovery and Quitting and Cleaning yourself up, or

O +N to Y, where +N offsets –N, as Support, as, for example, an intervention by loved ones, or a support group such as Alcoholics Anonymous, or treatment by a therapist.

The Low Self-Esteem Spiral:

Y –N to Y as Self-destructive Action (treating yourself like a piece of trash) for –SE as Low Self-Esteem (feeling like your self-worth equals a piece of trash),

Y –SE to Y as Low Self-Esteem for Y –N to Y as Action

Cycle, and N increases with each cycle, until:

Death or a total nervous breakdown, or

Y +N to Y, where +N offsets –N, as taking steps to boost self-esteem and recover your pride in being yourself, such as some achievement or hobby, or

O +N to Y, where +N offsets –N, as Support, as, for example, support by loved ones, or a support group, or treatment by a therapist.

SE is the +N or –N that you expect, so:

Early success causes +SE

+SE leads to +N to Y

+N to Y leads to +SE

It becomes like a plane taking off from a runway.

Early failure causes –SE,

–SE causes a loss of self-confidence as inability to trust yourself or give yourself a loan,

–SE causes failure = –N to Y

–N to Y causes –SE to Y

So early failure can cause a downward spiral, like a plane where one engine fails and then the plane crashes.

This is why early success is so important to long-term success. If you have early failure and spiral down, the solution is to catch yourself before you crash, forgive all –N = Zero, then try again to have a small success as a source of +SE, and then build on whatever small successes you have to rebuild +SE to the point where your self-confidence would enable bigger successes = +N to Y, and then get back on the track of the "upward spiral" of +N for +SE, +SE for +N.

THE URGENTLY FELT MOST PRESSING EMOTIONAL NEED

Every human being's most urgent emotional need:

+N to Y for –N to Y

Support, comforting, justice, help, validation, vindication.

O is nice to Y after Y's hardship, O helps Y clean up the mess and heal the pain, Y loves O for it. O makes Y feel better. After a cry, a hug. After a bloody fight, bandages. After a breakup, a new love. After stress and anxiety, comfort.

Every politician and advertiser wants to sell this. People just want sympathy, justice, or to feel better.

EXAMPLE: THE OFFICE

Some people are being mean to you at work. O –N to Y.

You resent them as a result. Y –N to O as Emotion for O –N to Y as Action.

So you get angry and are mean back at them. Y –N to O as Action for Y –N to O as Emotion.

Your being mean and angry at work makes the people at work hate you even more. O –N to Y for Y –N to O.

Repeat the cycle of O –N to Y for Y –N to O for O –N to Y until Sum(N) = Everyone at work hates you, you hate everyone, and you feel miserable at the office, or where N exceeds Point A where A = the amount of –N that triggers an explosive fight or violent confrontation.

The solution: Y F(–N) = Zero, then Y +N to O, until O +N to Y for Y +N to O.

Step 1: Forgive them. Forgiveness is key. Forgive, and really mean it. (The difference between forgiving negativity, on the one hand, and repressing or hiding from negative feelings and pretending you don't feel them, will be explained later. The TLDR is that with forgiveness, you forgive the moral debt they owe you, so you don't feel they owe you, so your negative emotion towards them ceasing to exist.)

Step 2: Be cheerful and friendly towards them. Even to the mean ones. Having forgiven them, you won't feel anger towards them, so you don't just pretend to be nice, and go through the motions. You have to really mean it.

Step 3: Eventually, this "remedial" being nice will change the perception of you at the office. People will like you. And then they will be friendly to you, because they like you. Maybe some of the really mean, rude ones will still hate you. But you will just forgive them, every time, and so it won't affect or impact your office cheerfulness and friendliness, which will make any normal person or group of people like you.

THE STORE CLERK: AN ETIQUETTE STORY

X walks into Store A. There he meets Store Clerk A.

Clerk A tells X about Rule A. For example, no T-shirts or sandals allowed in the store. And X is wearing a T-shirt and sandals. But that is only one possible example; for another example, maybe X had an appointment to pick something up at the store, and X is five minutes late, so A has to tell X that X is too late and X has to return tomorrow to pick up his package. Or maybe customers aren't allowed to bring food into the store, and X brought some food, and A has to tell X to throw it out or else leave. Any example of –N to X as a customer in a store works.

A seeks to enforce Rule A against X. A asks X to comply or else to leave the store.

This is: A –N to X.

What happens next:

Either:

X complies. X +N to A as compliance, X +N to X as enjoying the store.

Or:

X gets angry. X –N back to A.

Then A gets angry in response to X's anger. A –N to X.

Next:

Either:

X –N to A and A –N to X until N escalates to the level where they have a fight,

Or:

A tells X to leave immediately.

Then:

Either:

X leaves. X cuts losses where loss to X = A –N to X. –N to X is capped at whatever level it was at the point at which X left.

Or:

A kicks X out. A –N to X and A cuts losses where loss to A = X –N to A. Then all future –N to A from X is capped at past levels.

Or:

They argue, but A tries to be nice and respectful to X as A +N to X, X feels appreciated and respected and reciprocates with respect = X +N to A, then their argument takes the form of a peaceful debate about Rule A, and then X agrees to peacefully:

Either:

Comply: X +N to X as stay and enjoy, X +N to A as comply and end making a scene in the store.

Leave: X +N to A as respect, X +N to X as get whatever relief comes of getting out of that situation.

In this situation, it is a cost-benefit analysis for A and X of how they can maximize +N to them. X wants to wear a T-shirt and sandals, but X also wants to enjoy shopping in the store. A wants to enforce the rules that it is part of A's job to enforce, but A also doesn't want to make a scene in the store and make other shoppers uncomfortable. Social Skills and social IQ, in this situation, is reading the other person's motives, and using +N to the other person as Speech (as politeness, respect, de-escalation) to try to get the other person to make a decision that you can win under.

If X chooses to leave, there is often:

The Parting Shot:

X rude to A on the way out: X –N to A where A cannot be rude as –N back to X (because X has left).

Then A –N to X as Emotion (futile frustration or anger), which A might then misdirect and vent at other customers, or A F(–N) = Zero to X and just forget the whole thing and move onto the next customer with a cheerful emotional state.

Or:

A rude to X as X exits: A –N to X that X can't repay/retaliate, because X just left.

Then X –N to A as Emotion (frustration, anger), which X might redirect and vent at any random person who is nearby or by being angry at life in general, or X F(–N) = Zero to A, and just move on with a clear mind and a clean soul.

Instead of The Parting Shot, sometimes, there is The Parting Forgiveness:

A F(–N) to X, and A is polite and friendly to X as X leaves, as A +N to X to repay A –N to X.

And/or:

X F(–N) to A, X is polite to A while X exits, as X +N to A to offset X –N to A as refusal or unwillingness to comply and inconvenience to A as store employee.

But, if X stays, this might happen:

A F(–N) to X and A gives good customer service as A +N to A for X + $N to A as X spends money and shops and buys stuff from A,

Or:

A Hide(–N) to X as resentment, for example, the waitress giving the "sneeze muffin" to the customer she doesn't like, that she sneezed on it behind the counter out of sight, and then serves it to him.

And:

X F(–N) to A, for example X leaves a tip + $N to A as a symbol of X +N to A to show appreciation and support,

Or:

X Hide(–N) to A, for example leaves a negative online review of A's store, or calls A's manager the next day to complain about A's service.

If X complies and chooses to remain, and if A intends to be nice to X, A will read X's body language to determine whether X wants A to hover over X and say nice things and make small talk, or whether this makes X feel self-conscious and awkward and X would rather be left alone to shop while being ignored by A. Thus, the behavior that X wants is how A can express +N to X, but there is no "one size fits all" of what is +N, instead A has to read X, and then what X happens to want is what gives +N to X. Or, of course, if A resentfully wants to give some pain to X, giving X whatever X doesn't want is –N to X, if X doesn't want hovering and constant friendly small talk or if X doesn't want to be left alone and ignored.

To begin this story at the end, with a "prequel," A is aware that all of this might happen, so, in order for A to approach X and ask X to comply and inform X of Rule A, knowing that a confrontation and fallout might occur,

A Loans +N to A as Courage such that +N Exceeds –N where –N = A's Fear of X –N to A.

But in this case, in this story, it has a happy ending, because A is perfectly polite to X and A displays respect for X when A approaches X and asks X to comply with Rule A, A is so nice and friendly that X wants to reciprocate by complying to make life easier for X (and so that X can enjoy this store, which seems nice and good-looking), it turns out that this is a clothing store, and X buys a long-sleeved shirt and shoes and immediately puts them on, thereby complying with the no T-shirts and no sandals rule, A is friendly and warm and nice to X while X shops in the store, and X leaves a $5 tip for A as a sign of emotional appreciation and joy.

Add this detail to the middle of the story:

X chooses to stay in the store, and X is shopping.

A is helping other customers. X signals to A that X needs A's help.

A keeps X waiting. A is helping someone else and this other customer is very needy and is taking a lot of time for A to help them.

X doesn't like to wait. X is kept waiting for a long time. X feels that this behavior is A –N to X as Action.

X gets angry. X –N to A as Emotion.

So what happens next?

Either:

X screams at A "Hey, hello over there! I'm waiting! I've been waiting a really long time!" as rudeness = X –N to A as Action.

Or X F(–N) A, and X politely waits, to be nice.

What does A do if X is rude to A?

This is the key to great customer service.

This is what A should not do: A can –N to X as Action as A being rude back to X, saying "I'm sorry, sir, you are just going to have to wait your turn, these other customers need help also, please wait," in a nasty tone.

Then X –N to A as rudeness back, A –N to X as rudeness back for that, and the interaction collapses. It becomes a contest to see if one person's –N to the other person exceeds the –N the other person directs back at them. The "winner" is the person who delivers the biggest –N as rudeness, anger, aggression, and that person feels they established dominance over the other person, because their –N was bigger.

This is what A should do:

A F(–N) = Zero to X. A should just forgive X, instantly and completely. And then be pleasant, nice, and friendly back to X. A shouldn't just fake being nice. A can really mean it. Because A has forgiven X, A feels no emotion of anger towards X.

Then A helps the other customers, but A runs over and tries to help X also at the same time, and A does A's best to help X as soon as possible, or apologizes in a nice, friendly, polite tone. X may appreciate it. Or X may still feel that A hasn't helped X enough. But A +N to X as being friendly and polite and nice and cheerful is the best way to get X to spend +$N in A's store. That is what A earns a salary equal to +$N in return for doing: forgiving X, being nice to X, and giving great customer service (meaning: polite, friendly) to X.

But this requires A to have the maturity to forgive, instead of getting angry, and then getting sucked into the power struggle for dominance of who can assert more rudeness and anger as –N against the other person and get away with it. If A forgives X, then it doesn't matter how much anger, rudeness, aggression, or dominance X asserts to A as –N, the size of X's –N to A doesn't matter, because A F(–N) = Zero, A forgives X's anger, rendering it a nullity.

MASON JONES: A STORY ABOUT RECOVERY

Let M = Mason Jones (he/they)

M is a soldier in a war.

M and M's friend are soldiers on the battlefield.

M's friend dies in combat, M tries to save him but cannot. M survives.

M –N to M as Emotion: Guilt where N = Value of Friend's Life (Survivor's Guilt). M subconsciously/emotionally blames self for friend's death, and M's life is a symbol of blame = Guilt where –N = the value of a human life. So M feels that M deserves to die, where M –N to M for M –N to M's friend.

M uses drugs and alcohol as +N to M as Emotion (pleasure of drugs and alcohol) where –N Guilt = +N drugs.

M drugs and alcohol Hide(–N Guilt = Survivor's Guilt) as numbness/painkilling +N.

M –N to M as Emotion: Guilt as feeling guilty about using drugs and alcohol.

M drugs and alcohol Hide(–N Guilt = guilt from addiction).

Repeat: M uses drugs and alcohol to Hide(–N as Guilt from using drugs and alcohol).

Cycle as Sum(–N as Guilt) grows itself.

M –SE = Sum(–N).

M tries to get sober.

M sober for Time T = +N.

M –SE = M expects to not deserve M +N to M, so +N to M causes M –N to M as Guilt for M +N to M.

Net result of being sober is –N to M as Guilt ("I'm not a good person, sober me is not the real me, I'm only human and imperfect.")

M uses drugs and alcohol to Hide this M –N to M.

Repeat/Cycle for each attempt to sober up.

Then M –N to M as Guilt for each failure to sober up or stay sober.

Repeat/Cycle.

Then one of two things happen:

Repeat/Cycle until Sum(–N) = M –N to M where N is an amount equal to death or total collapse and self-annihilation of any attempt to live a normal healthy happy life. Punishment for being alive as drugs and alcohol, punishment for being an addict and alcoholic as drugs and alcohol, punishment for being sober and trying to be a better person than you feel you really are as drugs and alcohol.

Or:

M files for Moral Bankruptcy.

M F(–N) to M = Zero for: drugs and alcohol, failure to be perfect and failed sobriety, having not been able to save his friend and still being alive.

M owes MD(Zero) to M: M does not owe drugs and alcohol use to himself as punishment.

M owes Zero to M as Emotion: End of emotional pain and guilt. A fresh start.

M sobers up.

M enters Rehab and AA, where group therapy and moral support equals +N to counter and offset –N to M that can manifest as addiction.

M F(–N as Emotion: Shame stigma embarrassment of being an addict) to enable M to have the courage to face Rehab/AA and to keep going without embarrassment or shame.

M builds back M's life, by M +N to M, where Sum(+N) = Rebuilding life.

M achieves Goal G = Sobriety.

M achieves Goals G = Get a job, get married, have kids, climb Mount Everest.

M +N to M as Emotion: Happiness for M +N to M as Achieved Goal G = Rebuilt Life, Live Life.

M, with a friend from AA, visits the cemetery where his friend from the war is buried. M leaves a wreath of flowers at the friend's grave. M cries. M leans on his AA friend's shoulder, and sobs in tears. M cries until all the tears are gone.

M leaves the cemetery.

M lives his life. Without guilt. Without pain. Without drug addiction and alcoholism.

Without the downward spiral of cycle/repeat –N as Action, for –N as Emotion, for –N as Action, for –N as Emotion, to infinity, until death.

MOISHE GOLDSTEIN: A STORY ABOUT SELF-ESTEEM

Let M = Moishe Goldstein (he, him, his)

M is a math and science genius in high school. M is proud of being so smart. M uses his high IQ as the basis of his self-esteem, as a young man. M has high self-esteem because of his very high IQ.

M gets into an Ivy League college named X.

M is from a poor family. $N limits scope of N. M's family cannot afford tuition for X.

M is rejected for a scholarship due to bad luck. The school runs out of grants before they reach his application.

M has to go to a low-ranked state college instead. The state school gives an in-state tuition discount and a grant.

M –N to M as Guilt where N = value of Ivy League status to M's self-esteem SE.

X as a symbol of IQ as a basis of SE. Absence of X as a basis of low self-esteem = M –SE to M.

M uses alcohol as –N to M as punishment for Blame = –N for X.

M –N to M as alcoholism for P(M –N to M as Action as not being good enough or smart enough to go to X).

M alcoholic behavior –N to O (to everyone around him, including at work) as M –N to M for M –N to M.

M's drunken anger as M –N to O for M –N to M.

M alcoholic crazy stupid behavior as M –$N to M as M ruining M's career.

M –$N to M as symbol of M –N to M to punish M for M –N to M as failure to get into X.

M gets a civil engineer license and gets a job as a civil engineer, because his genius is evident, even though everyone knows he is an alcoholic.

M is an alcoholic and gets drunk daily and gets angry and engages in self-destructive behavior daily.

M goes to parties. He gets drunk. He gets angry at everyone (himself and everyone else). He pukes all over. He drunkenly passes out. He wakes up on the street, or in some random motel room naked, or at home while still wearing his vomit-stained clothes.

M is drunk and angry. M meets some random stranger at a bar one night. M is complaining to everyone near enough to hear him about how unfair life is. The stranger hears M complain about M's life story. The stranger immediately understands M. The stranger explains to M that M needs to forgive M for his failure to go to an Ivy League college as a symbol of his low self-esteem, and that self-forgiveness will set M free from anger, shame and guilt. This stranger explains the math and logic behind this. The stranger finishes his beer, and leaves. M never sees him or meets him ever again. M ever doesn't learn the stranger's name.

M wakes up, hung over and with beer-stained clothes, the next morning. But he remembers what the stranger told him. He wakes up that morning sober, and he understands. He chooses not to drink that day.

M F(–N = X) for M, M F(Blame M), M F(–N = career failure).

M F(–N = Indicia of Low or Average IQ).

M recovers +SE = High science and math IQ as basis of SE as "I am a smart, intelligent, good person."

M recovers High IQ = High SE Basis = M +N to M as career achievement.

M sobers up. M stops drinking. Permanently.

M, in order to get back in the habit of doing high-level civil engineering work, takes up a hobby of reviewing the blueprints and engineering plans of local buildings, to look for ways to improve them and sell himself as an applicant by mentioning his ideas for this to local architecture firms.

M reviews the local building blueprints on record in the public records file at M's local Town Hall.

M notices something. Something bad. Something scary.

The much-hyped new development the Super Skyscraper Skyrise has an engineering flaw.

It was based on a 100-story building that was built in California.

It is going to be built in New York.

When winter comes, in a blizzard, with snow and high winds, its roof will collapse.

In California, this design never had blizzards.

No one noticed. Everyone just assumed that, because the California architect was famous and a genius, that it would be fine. No one carefully double-checked every detail of the design against pressure from intense heavy snow plus high wind gusts. No one understood the weight of snow plus the pressure of intense wind at precisely the right place in in the blueprint to crush the roof.

The building is being built by a famous New York architecture firm. Their engineers examined the blueprints. They just didn't notice. They assumed. They didn't understand how wind and snow could combine. M's science and civil engineering brain immediately understood after he looked at the blueprints. Then he did the math. He has proof.

A billion dollars is invested in this office building. M's local town is counting on it to revitalize their downtown economy. So much was riding on this building.

Construction is 75% complete. $750 million has been spent.

What has been built is worthless. Unsafe. It has to be torn down. And rebuilt.

M says this to the Town's civil engineering safety commission.

The building developer begins a smear campaign against M. Calls him an alcoholic. A loser. A liar. He wants to finish the building.

The developer petitions the civil engineering board to have M's license revoked.

The board holds a joint hearing, on M's license and the building's permit.

The developer's lawyers ask M about M's education. M answers calmly. Without anger. Any trade of anger will confirm the rumors. M would lose at trial. M stays calm. He feels no anger. "But you didn't get into X, did you? "No." "You're not an Ivy League graduate, are you?" "No." "You went to that crappy local state school, didn't you?" "Yes." "And you don't work for a high-prestige firm, do you?" "No." "You have caused minor disturbances, while drunk, haven't you?" "Yes." "You have a reputation as the town drunk, don't you?"

"Objection." "Sustained. M seems reasonable. M, what is your proof?"

M calmly, clearly explains the math and science of the building's design flaw. He is happy to get to share his knowledge with people who want to learn. He explains. He is passionate. He is smiling. He proves his argument.

The developers' lawyers look at each other. The board are engineers themselves. They understand.

The lawyers know they've lost.

The building is scrapped and rebuilt. Hundreds of lives are saved as a result.

The case attracts national attention. M gets a reputation as a smart person.

A local, high-prestige engineering firm offers M a job.

M takes it.

M stays sober, has his self-esteem, is confident that he is smart, feels no blame and no guilt and no shame, is happy, works as a civil engineer doing big-money high-stakes work, continues to review local blueprints for flaws as a hobby, and lives a long and happy life.

ABNER AND XANDER: A FISH OUT OF WATER – A LOVE STORY

Let A = Abner Lewis (he, him, his)

Let X = Xander Willems (he/she/they)

At Time T = Past, someone A trusted, named person P (a parent, teacher, friend, coworker, lover, partner, spouse) was in A's life. P betrayed A = P –N to A. P told or implied to A that A was worthless. A –SE = –N at Time T = Now for P –N to A at Time T = Past.

A has low self-esteem. A feels stung and void because of P's betrayal. A hides the pain, frequently in beer. But the scar never healed, it was submerged in alcohol instead, like an iceberg beneath water.

A dates partner B.

A tried to derive self-esteem +SE = Value of B.

B's flaws = –N to A's SE.

B is not good enough for A.

A dumps and breaks up with B.

Repeat with person B2, person B3, person B4.

Cycle for person BN where N is the number of boyfriends A has previously broken up with for not being good enough for him.

A goes to a singles bar. The name of the bar is "A Fish Out of Water."

A sees X. X seems like the perfect person for A. X seems perfect.

A's stare meets X's gaze from across the bar. A stares into X's beautiful eyes. A instantly falls in love. A gazes longingly at X's beauty.

A P(X's value = High +N).

A doubts that A can seduce X. A isn't good enough. X is worth too high a price for A to pay. X is out of A's league.

A is at the bar that night with A's wingman, A's friend, D.

A points out X to D. D says go for it. A says he can't. He is too afraid. A isn't good enough for X.

D gives A this advice: Give him a loan. Give yourself a loan.

A says: What?

D explains: Give him a loan. Loan him the belief that he is the love of your life. That you and he will fall in love, marry, and live happily ever after. I know that you don't believe in love at first sight, Abner, but, for this guy, act like you believe in love at first sight, and that he is it. Talk to him and behave like you have fallen in love with him, from day one, from your first conversation with him. Love him that much. Be nice to him that much. Begin by believing that he is your soul mate, and love him, before you have gotten to know him. Then let that love happen during the relationship, naturally, as you get to know each other, after you have already believed it would come true. A loan of hope and trust and faith. A loan of love, repaid by being loved.

Give yourself a loan. Believe you can do this. Trust yourself, and have the self-confidence to do this. Know that you can do it. Know that you've got this. Then you'll actually find out whether you really can do it, later, after you have already done it. Loan yourself self-confidence today. Loan to yourself the knowledge that you will succeed. Then prove that the loan was justified, pay for it, repay it, tomorrow. With your successful relationship as the interest repaid to you on the loan capital.

A: Okay.

And then A downs a few beers, A does one shot of vodka to chase the beer down, and A goes over to X, and A initiates a conversation with X. A says hello, and starts talking, and makes a joke, and asks X what X's hobbies and interests are, and gets X talking to A. X is smart, funny, interesting, and shares a lot of the same interests as A. A and X get along very well together, and X thinks that A's jokes are funny. A flirts with X, A and X talk and laugh and make jokes, they have some drinks, A hits on X and A asks X to come home with him, X comes home with A, they hook up, and the next morning they eat breakfast together of coffee, toast, and scrambled eggs, at A's apartment, and they decide to date. They watch TV and cuddle together that night, and are inseparable thereafter. They are partners, lovers, and best friends, and they make each other incredibly happy.

X dates A.

A is happy. A +N to A as Emotion for A +N to A as Action as having won X for X +N to A as Action and Emotion as X's love and what a great guy X is and how much A likes X.

But then, as they get to know each other, A learns that X has a dark secret. A learns X's dark secret. X is imperfect. X has flaws. In this example, X is physically attractive, and X put himself through college and law school and paid for it by having a career as an adult film star and adult content creator. A is horrified when A learns this, and A now views X as dirty and trashy and horrible. X has been with hundreds of lovers. By contrast, A has only had less than a dozen lovers and partners in A's entire life.

A P(X's Flaws = N and X −N to A as −N to A's SE).

A confronts X, gets angry, and screams at X, in tears, while crying. A dumps X and breaks up with X, even though A loves X and X is the love of A's life.

A is sad. A –N to A as Emotion: depression for A –N to A as Emotion: Guilt for A –N to X as Action: Breaking up with X.

A is depressed. A gets drunk every day and is drunk 24/7 to kill the pain. A screams at D. A wakes up hung over, drenched in vomit and tears. A cries.

A goes to counseling. A's therapist explains the principles of moral psychology to A.

A F(X –N to A where N = X's imperfection).

A +SE = A F(A –N to A for the betrayal at Time T = Past) = Zero.

A now is not using X's value as a basis of A +SE. A isn't trying to use X +N to A as Value of X to compensate or repay for P –N to A at Time T = Past.

A loans +N to A for A apologize to X.

A meets X at the bar where they first met. They see each other from across the bar. They walk towards each other.

X cries, X hugs and kisses A, X and A reunite and get back together. X loves A. A loves X.

X has already forgiven A for breaking up with X, because X is emotionally mature and knows how to choose to forgive someone, like a true adult.

A +N to X as Love. X +N to A as Love. A as Debtor +N to A as Creditor as Happy Life for Loan = Courage to face X again after their fight.

A and X live a happy life together and having a loving romance and get married and have kids and grandkids and grow old together and live happily ever after.

DANIEL DOMINIC: A STORY ABOUT FORGIVENESS

Let D = Daniel Dominic (he, him, his)

D is a child.

D stands to inherit estate = $N from D's father.

D's father dies.

D's father leaves the estate to D's sister.

D Blames D's mother, who he thinks talked his father into it.

D –N to mother as anger, as Emotion.

D grows up and becomes a young adult.

D cuts D's mother out of D's life as D –N to mother as Action. D is originally from the South. D moves to the Northeast, away from all his Southern family and relatives.

D –N to Life as anger, Blaming Life in general for Life –N to D as Life (Life = bad luck, fate, the world, everyone) –$N to D.

D drinks an amount of alcohol = D –N as anger towards Life.

D has money trouble. He gets drunk a lot. He can't hold a job for long. He works as a carpenter and electrician and plumber.

D Blames problems on mother –$N to D.

D offloads Blame = −N from D onto D's parents.

D −N to mother for D +N to D as Not D −N to D as Blame.

D asks the bank for a loan. At first the bank says no. D is angry. D drinks his anger away.

A few months pass. Then the bank calls D. The bank is willing to offer a loan to D.

D gets a loan of $N(2). The bank says they gave D the loan because the loan was guaranteed by a pledge of collateral from a mysterious person, who does not choose to disclose their identity to D. D wonders if it is D's girlfriend, somehow, because she has a rich uncle, although D has never met him. But D doesn't mention it to his girlfriend.

D uses $N(2) to start a small business. Remodeling houses.

D succeeds in business. Small business Goal G is achieved by D.

G +$N to D. G +N to D as happiness. D forgives Life for some −N to D.

Time passes. D is now an adult.

D's money problems go away. D becomes happy. D marries his longtime girlfriend. They have three little kids together.

D decides it is time to travel home. To forgive D's mother.

D drives a long drive down to the South, in a pickup truck, with the windows down. It is summer.

D meets D's sister, at a restaurant as a neutral site, to confront her, and also to forgive her.

When she sees him, she expects him to scream at her. But he is perfectly polite and friendly to her. He seems relaxed. Not angry. He seems happy now.

D's sister explains that, because D was a child when D's father died, and a legal minor, had the estate been left to him in his father's will, the state could have seized it under state law. D's mother talked D's father into leaving it to D's sister, who was of the age of majority at that time, for D's benefit. D, as a little child, was too young to understand, and by the time had he grown up, he was too angry at them for them to talk to him about it. D's sister was the mystery loan guarantor to the bank, but she only helped D get the loan because D's mother told her to. D's mother was always just trying to save D financially. (D's sister doesn't personally like D all that much. But his mother loves him.)

D meets his mother, face to face, at their old estate mansion. They see each other for the first time in decades. She has grown old, ancient. Her skin is wrinkled. Her hair is gray.

What do you want from me? She asks him.

To forgive… his voice trails off.

I forgive you, she says.

Thanks, he manages to say, in a soft voice, struggling to speak through his emotions.

They hug. They have afternoon tea together on the patio. They cry. They hug again. He leaves. He returns home, to his business, and to his wife and kids, in the Northeast.

D $F(-N = \text{anger}) = \text{Zero}$. D forgives his mother, his father, his sister, and Life in general.

D stops drinking alcohol. D sobers up. D no longer needs the alcohol. D is no longer angry at Life.

D lives happily ever after.

HOW TO BE TAKEN SERIOUSLY

There are two human languages, in every language: LNS (Literal, Not Serious) Language, and SNL (Serious, Not Literal) Language. Whether you take what someone says literally, but not seriously, or whether you take them seriously, but not literally.

To tell whether someone likes you, it depends upon whether they communicate using LNS or SNL.

In LNS, you just ask "Hey, do you like me?" And they answer yes or no.

But, if they speak SNL, then asking "Hey, do you like me?" comes across as awkward and socially unskilled. It's too direct and abrupt.

In SNL, you read social cues, like body language, whether they laugh at your jokes or not, whether their eyes light up when they see you or they roll their eyes when they see you, whether they go out of their way to meet you or go out of their way to make excuses to avoid being at events you are at.

Do they look happy when they see you?

Do they make eye contact with you?

Do they avoid you?

You can also make a "symbolic gesture" to ask them whether they like you, and then interpret their answer. For example, ask them to dinner one on one, or ask them to see a movie with you. Make sure you are alone with them when you ask, so there is no social pressure on them, from your group of friends or such. They should give you an honest answer of yes or not, which can represent their answer to the question: Do you like me?

SNL is Huff, snort, moan, sigh Language:

Huff/snort: O –N to Y

Moan: O –N to O for Y

Sigh: O P(Y –N to O or Life –N to O)

Often, LNS is socially inappropriate and looks awkward and comes across as harsh. Saying the same thing in SNL looks normal and appropriate.

LNS states literal meaning. SNL states by implication of an indirect statement or inference from tone and body language. SNL sugar-coats the message with +N to O, because you don't have to hear the harshness and cruelty of the literal meaning, you just see it implied softly.

Consider these statements, which sound rude in LNS, but are frequently stated in SNL:
"I want to have sex with you tonight."

"Do you like me?"

"I don't like you."

"I think that I am superior to you." "I think that I am smarter than you."

"I don't want to see you or spend time with you." "I don't want you to be around me."

These are implied, and you take the hint or get the message in SNL, which you translate into LNS in your own mind to understand the literal meaning of what was implied. You should never say any of these out loud, because they are huge –N to Others. But, if you think them, you can imply them, and you should always listen for them. You can't say such things because it looks bad, but if you state them in SNL then there is nothing there to see so nothing looks bad.

Some people, for example, feel that sexuality is gross, so they don't want to directly address any statement that involves sex (or dating and romance, to the extent those involve sex), so you can't say anything about sex to them directly, but if you imply it and discuss it in SNL then they can talk about it without having to directly or consciously face it and feel grossed out by it. They want sex, but they don't want to have to think about it or talk about it.

This is true for any ugly truth, such as one person hating or disliking another person, especially for an unpleasant reason such as arrogance/sense of superiority. A person can believe that they are better than other people, but that is a cruel truth to face, so people want to imply it without ever directly saying it, if they want to say it at all.

If X says that X is better than A in LNS, that is seen as X –N to A as arrogance (or as racism or as sexism, etc.), for which any listener or audience out of a sense of justice will impose –N to X as Judgment and Shame on behalf of A.

But if X says the same thing in SNL, listeners are not confronted with the thing that X has meant, so they don't feel (or feel to a lesser extent) a need to punish X with –N to X for A as condemnation.

Taken to an extreme, one could say everything in SNL, which is what politicians do, using nothing but double-speak and never saying anything literally because any literal meaning that they assert would offend one or more groups of voters with a sense of judgment against the politician. But then, if you only use SNL and never assert literal plain honest truth in LNS, people might judge you for that overuse of SNL, too, much as some people view politicians as tactful but dishonest.

HOW TO CLOSE
A DEAL

There are five types of businesspeople in this world, when it comes to making deals:

(1) The ones who want Y +N to O. So you take them to the right restaurant, buy them the right bottle of wine, buy the right gift for their spouse, meet them at a meet-and-greet at the right business conference at the right resort hotel, get a personal reference from the right friend of theirs, say the right things, and look good, attractive, normal, and be perfectly polite and well-spoken and sophisticated, and have the right picture-perfect spouse and kids that you have pictures of on your desk, and hang the right impressive high-pedigree diploma on the wall, and work in the right nice-looking office filled with beautiful people when they visit your office for a meeting to discuss the deal, and all that. What they want is +N to them from you, as sensations of pleasure from doing business with you, and the more +N you give to them, the more likely they are to close the deal. This is what it means to say that you want them to form the right impression of you as someone they want to do business with.

(2) The ones who want Y +$N to O. They are looking to make money. They don't care about politeness or rudeness. They don't want attractiveness or beauty or pleasant sensations. They care only about money. You could be polite or rude, or look professional or amateur. They don't care. What matters is your proof, in numbers and data, about how much cash the deal

will bring in for them. That proof, and only that proof, is what persuades them.

(3) The ones who want O –N to Y. They want to be mean to you and be rude to you and make you jump through hoops and accept inconveniences which they impose upon you, in order to establish their dominance over you, as a symbol of O –N to Y. They want you to let them display –N as their aggression towards you. If you submit, and they feel that they own you, that is when they will do the deal. They want to be the "alpha wolf," and the more you enable that, the more you are likely to close the deal. Your +N to them, your actually being nice or trying to look professional or good-looking to them, won't be noticed, other than that they read it as a sign of weakness. The story comes to mind (and this is a true story) of the Silicon Valley software tycoon mogul who would demand of people that they discuss business deals while naked together in his giant jacuzzi bathtub with him at his Silicon Valley mansion, and he would walk away from the deal if they said no, as the classic example. The other person wants to feel a sense of power over you, so you let them, to get the deal. So you essentially pay for O +\$N to Y with O –N to Y, if you feel that is what you want to do, possibly with Y F(Y –N to Y for O –N to Y) = Zero, that you forgive yourself for feeling dirty that you let them do that do you in order to close the deal, which is the adult mature choice, if you had to do it financially. They want to dominate, and they want you to submit. But doing this for the deal, doesn't mean you have done it for your soul. Their dominance ends when you leave work and go home for the day. You don't take it home with you. If you feel angry or resentful at home, after work, because of how this person treated you, then you should forgive yourself. You did what you had to do, or, if you wanted the deal to close, then you did what you wanted to do. If it reaches that point, you have to decide whether it is really worth it, and when to walk away. Some people have situations where they need the deal to close, and the other person is that type of person. Then what is very useful to

you is: F(O –N to Y) = Y owes Zero (forgive yourself = no shame, no guilt) to Y and Y owes Zero to O (forgive them = no anger, no resentment). It should be just about the money, in business. You shouldn't take it personally. Then your emotions won't hurt you. Submitting in this context is not Y +N to O. Submitting in this context is Y –N to Y for O +$N to Y. What they want is a detriment to you, not a benefit for them. It is inherently negative and self-destructive, not positive and life-affirming. But some people, in business, ask for, expect, and demand this. As will be discussed in this book, some people use –N, instead of +N, to get what they want out of people, as a social skills strategy, and such people will enjoy O –N to Y, with their leverage of Y wanting or needing to close a deal. But you are free to choose to seek to close a deal with such a person. Then, to get what you want in business, the math is Y –N to Y for O +$N to Y for Y +N to Y. The happiness you give yourself from success in business, by means of submitting on a selective basis, exceeds the emotional pain, or hit that your self-esteem takes, or damage to your pride, from demeaning or belittling yourself for someone else, to close the deal and make the sale.

(4) The next type in business are the ones who will test you with O –N to Y as rudeness and aggression, because they are looking to see if you will fight back with Y –N to O by being angry and assertive back at them, or whether you will respond with Y F(–N) = Zero or Y Hide(–N to Y) and then Y +N to O as being polite and nice and friendly back at them and ignoring their rudeness and mistreatment of you, because they want to see how you will react in a fight, to see how tough you are, to see whether they want to do a deal with you. If you handle their –N well, with grace, depending on whether they had wanted to see –N to O (fight back) or +N to O (forgive, shrug it off, and be nice and friendly and polite) as your reply, that will make them see you as someone, as the type of person, that they want to close a deal with. So the math looks like: O +N to Y as Respect for Y –N to O as Pushback and Assertiveness for O –N to Y as Rudeness

or Aggression or Domination. Or: O +N to Y as Appreciation and Being Impressed for Y +N to O as Being Cheerful and Polite and Calm and Nice for O –N to Y as Rudeness or Aggression or Domination. Of course, obviously, O has been rude to Y, and that's not nice of O, even if O did it just to test Y and see how Y reacts. It would be normal for Y to get angry at O, or, if Y is not allowed to express anger at O because then Y loses the deal, it is normal for Y to repress and for Y to get angry at Y because of O. If Y represses anger, then Y's politeness seems forced and unnatural, or the anger builds up and then Y explodes and Y is openly rude to O, and then all prospects of a deal are gone, because O takes offense and walks away. But Y can forgive O, instead of getting angry and repressing anger or exploding in anger. Because Y is a mature adult. So Y is the master of Y's emotions, and Y doesn't care. If Y truly forgives, then Y isn't angry. Y does, in fact, wish positive energy and good vibes to O, regardless of O's behavior. Then Y's +N can be sincere and honest, and will come across as such. That is what impresses and earns respect. If you are a nice person, people will like you. And that helps Y get the deal closed. In this scenario.

(5) The last type of person in business is the one who will mix the first four types. One common combo is type one plus type two, so they want you to be polite and attractive and good-looking and classy and business-savvy and have great business professional etiquette, but they also want to be persuaded that the deal will bring them a huge amount of money and profit. Or someone could combine types three and four, that they will try to dominate you, and want to, but if you put up a fight and resist and fight back, that impresses them and causes them to respect you. Or, as is common in business, the decision to close a deal will be made, not by one person, but by a committee or group or board of directors, and each member might have one of these five styles, so that a combination of styles will evaluate you to decide to close the deal.

It's really important, to close a deal, that, as soon as

possible, you identify which of these five types of styles you are dealing with, so that way you know what to focus on in order to close the deal, but giving the decision-maker what they want to have to persuade them to decide to choose your deal, and not all the other potential suitors offering deals to them. And if you are wrong about what the other person wants, you might give them the wrong thing, and so lose the deal. So you have to read the other person continuously to see what it is that they want, to make sure you have not misread them and given them the wrong thing and that you are giving them what they want to close the deal. You should also try to seek out favorable matchups, such as, for example, that the math and science geek who knows hard numbers does better proving a profit equal to +$N, and the really handsome or beautiful nice person who is well-schooled in fancy restaurants and expensive wines and resort hotels and who is fun to be around and who can be the life of the party does better at giving +N.

In dealmaking there is often a scenario where the other person gives –N to you as them trying to force you to accept deal terms favorable to them and unfavorable to your side. The question is, do you push back, with your –N towards them, because if you don't they will take every advantage they can get and take the shirt off your back, but, if you do push back, if your –N offends them they may walk away from the deal completely. How much –N to give back is a judgment call, for you to make as a negotiator and dealmaker, that for the most part depends on what deal terms your business requires from the other person in order to make a profit. You demand the terms you need, and walk away if you don't get them. You concede the terms you don't need or want, to be nice and polite. And then it's a judgment call how big of a fight to put up for deal terms in the gray area of what you want but don't absolutely need. Deals fall through because one side pushed too much, all the time. But deals also happen where one side gets less than they could have gotten or should have gotten. Again, it is a judgment call for you as negotiator and businessperson. And then there is the classic technique of trading $-N$ in one area of the deal terms in return for $+N$ in another area of the deal terms, which you can do.

If the deal falls though, and you get blamed for that, it will look like you $-N$ to your own business where N = the value of that deal to the business. If you boss won't forgive you, and you can't plausibly blame it on someone else, then the thing to do is to accept it with honor and apologize to your company as you $+N$ to them for the $-N$ to them that you caused. So, for your own point of view, you have to compare the other deal party's $-N$ to you in dealmaking, against the $-N$ your boss and your business will give you if you fail to make the deal and fail to close the deal.

MEN AND WOMEN

Definitions:

G: Any Goal, any end result or goal or objective that a person seeks or desires to obtain. Any goal that Y or O pursue.

Anger, aggression, force:

Y seeks Goal G from O by Y −N to O Exceeds O −N to Y.

The primary quality for causing −N is strength, to cause −N to O, and toughness to withstand pain, to accept −N from O without yielding to O. These are often thought of as a man's virtues. As such, the path of aggression and force is often associated with masculinity.

Attractiveness, pleasantness, trade:

Y seeks Goal G from O by O +N to Y as G for Y +N to O.

The primary qualities for causing +N are attractiveness, beauty, social skills, and emotional IQ. These are often thought of as a woman's virtues. As such, the path of attractiveness and beauty is often associated with femininity.

Trade, in economics, is often considered masculine, but peacefulness is seen as feminine, and trade is the inherently peaceful way to seek G, in contrast to force, which is the inherently warlike or argumentative way to seek G.

The paradigmatic relationship of man to woman is

Woman +N to Man for Man –N to Enemies where Man's –N to Enemies Exceeds Enemies –N to Woman. The man uses aggression and strength to protect the woman from their enemies, and the woman is nice to the man in return and gives beauty and pleasantness to the man in return.

This is the model of gender that existed for cavemen in the last Ice Age, and during the Dark Ages and ancient times. The prototypical, paradigmatic caveman model is that:

the man hunts for food, by hunting animals, (aggression)

and he fights other men, if they threaten or approach the woman, (toughness)

and he fends off predators, by fighting off wild animals, (strength)

while, in return,

the woman gives the man sex, (beauty, attractiveness)

and she raises the children, (social skills and emotional IQ)

and the woman gives emotional support to the man (social skills and emotional IQ)

and she keeps the man happy. (pleasantness)

So the man needs strength and aggression and toughness, and the woman needs beauty, social skills, and being emotionally adept.

The mathematical formula: Woman +N to Man for Man –N to Enemies.

Woman loves man, and her love forms their family, and, in return, man protects woman from their shared common enemies, man protects woman from danger, and man fights battles for woman.

Women would express their emotions, as +N to Man or as Woman's Need for +N from Man, but a man would not express his emotions, because this would be perceived as a sign of weakness, as Man –N to Man as Getting Emotional and being Vulnerable for Man +N to Man as being Emotionally sensitive and Managing his Emotions. Any sign of –N to Man would be interpreted as a sign of weakness, that would lessen the degree to which Man –N to Enemies Exceeds Enemies –N to Man. So women are thought of as emotional, while men are thought of as tough. Women always tell men to ask for help, but a man never wants to be helped in order to do something, because needing help is a sign of weakness, and a man always wants to be strong.

However, in modern times, anyone: man, woman, or any person, of any gender, can choose to use +N as a tool to achieve Goal G, or could choose to wield –N as a tool for seeking Goal G. They are not inherently limited to either gender, at least not in today's world. +N is the path of peaceful trade of value for value, of getting what you want by being good-looking and attractive and being nice and polite to people. –N is the path of getting into a fight in order to win and to conquer.

In traditional times, men used muscle to defeat their enemies. In modern times, a new type of man has emerged: the masculine nerd geek, who uses his brainy intelligence and his high IQ, instead of his muscles, to cause –N to his enemies, such as, for example, by devising schemes and plans to cause pain to his enemies, or by using his intelligence to figure out a way to defeat his enemies. A businessperson or lawyer, for example, wins in business, or in court, not by punching his enemy in the face and beating them up, but by outsmarting them, by making sales and crafting advertising campaigns, or by filing the correct motions and persuading a judge. The businessperson's success comes at the expense of his direct competitors, just as the lawyer's victory comes at the expense of his trial adversary, so those are fights, but fought with IQ, not with muscle.

In today's world, the attribute of causing –N to others has also served men well in business, and in sports, both of which can be viewed as competitions where you win by inflicting more –N onto your opponents than the amount of –N they inflicted onto you, such that If Y –N to O Exceeds O –N to Y, Then Y wins. It is a contest where the size of –N matters, and the biggest –N wins.

This may explain why business, and sports, are often male-dominated. A woman could succeed, in business, or in sports, but, to enjoy great success, she would have to win by inflicting –N onto her enemies, not by exceeding others' +N with her +N. Because that is how you win in a fight. And professional sports, and competition in free market capitalist business, are, ultimately, types of fights. You fight the other team to score more points. Or you fight the other competing businesses in your market for market share.

This book explains ways to defuse fights by means of projecting +N and Forgiveness of –N, but that doesn't "win the fight," it instead causes the two people to not have a fight. The focus of this book is on social skills, and using +N to achieve Goals, so the strategy and tactics to win by means of –N are not discussed in this book. But a person has to understand the +N and –N psychological dynamics, in order to read how people are behaving in a social situation, whether someone is trying to use +N, or whether someone is looking to have a fight and wield –N. There are situations where +N can defeat –N if the size of the +N Exceeds the size of the –N directed against it. The light of your positive energy outshines the darkness of their evil. However, if you face someone using negativity to achieve their goals, and if your +N does not Exceed their –N, if they are more negative than you are positive about whatever is involved, and if you are not willing to actually have a fight and have your –N Exceed their –N by being more mean and rude and angry and cruel and nasty and abusive and insulting than they are, then the other option is to walk away from that situation. Those are the three choices you have, most of the time: use +N, use –N, or walk away. Your approach should be that you should read the situation, and then choose the best option from among those three choices to achieve your Goals.

Insecurity about being a man or being a woman, and how this can be exploited psychologically for manipulation, is discussed elsewhere in this book.

Definitions:

Aggression: The willingness to seek out and engage in risks and dangers without fear, under the belief that you can cause an –N that exceeds the –N that can be done to you.

Strength: The ability to cause –N to Enemies. For example, being able to craft mean, hurtful insults and formulate verbal abuse.

Toughness: The ability to withstand –N that Enemies cause to You, without crumbling or giving in or being defeated. For example, the ability to be verbally insulted in a brutal, hurtful way, without really caring about it and without feeling pain or suffering from it.

Assertiveness: the quality of trying to take control of any situation you are in, and to assert yourself and assert your beliefs and goals and desires onto any situation.

Attractiveness: The ability to give +N to the Other. For example, beauty as a set of sensations that cause pleasure.

Social IQ: The ability to manage a trade of +N for +N, or of +N to O for O –N to Enemies. The ability to manage emotions and expectations in a long-term relationship, for example.

Positivity: The ability to cause +N in general, to both Self and Others. Being nice, for example.

"The men fight while the women flirt." Or, to quote the rock band Garbage, "The boys wanna fight while the girls just want to dance all night." Given the textbook caveman gender roles of Woman +N to Man for Man –N to Enemies (man fights other men, fights predators, hunts food, for woman), we can see that, in the traditional gender roles social and social psychological dynamic, Assertiveness and Aggression and Toughness and Strength are Masculine virtues, for Men, because they are used to win a fight, while attractiveness, social IQ, and positivity, are Feminine virtues, for Women, because these are what Women need to survive and trade in return by getting the Men to protect them and fight their battles for them.

Obviously, in Third Millennium Earth, with our modern contemporary progressive views on gender, this traditional caveman view of gender is laughable and absurd. But, still, the role of Man and the role of Woman in this social dynamic does still explain a great deal about the actual behavior of men and women in real life. Whenever the size of –N to challenged, whenever a man's –N is challenged, he will fight back, and resist, against any perceived force that seeks to demean his manhood. Women tend to become insecure in, and can be goaded into compensating for, their ability to give +N, for example insecurity about their beauty, or fear of a failure in social skills, such as not being popular.

But "man" and "woman," in this sense, are gender roles that any human person can perform, such as, for example, women in women's sports causing –N to the other team in a fight to win a game, or women in business using their high IQ to cause –N to win economic wars against competing businesses in their marketplaces, are women winning in a man's fight, or men in fashion and beauty industries being good at causing +N, or men as actors in the theater or movies known for their good looks, are men succeeding in a woman's industry. But you would tend to see men who perform the male gender role to gravitate towards and be more interested in areas where –N causes success, like sports (strength to cause –N) or business and technology (where high IQ is used to cause –N to opponents), and women who perform the female gender role as more interested in areas where attractiveness leads to success, like getting married and raising a family or child education (where teaching social IQ to children causes success) or customer service or fashion or music or internet/social media (where producing +N for an audience causes success).

In politics, the Right tends to be the more Manly, Masculine side. The Right value strength, and assertiveness, and domination against enemies (in foreign policy and wars, for example), and they view government control and regulations as a challenge to their manhood as the king of their household and independent ruler of their own life, and they value the toughness to be resilient against pain and to take a beating without getting knocked down.

In contrast, the Left tends to be more on the Womanly, Female side. The Left wants everyone to be taken care of and that no one should ever have to take risks or face danger, and everyone must always be protected by someone else (by the government), and they want everyone to always be treated in a nice respectful way, with people not being allowed to ever be mean or rude or disrespectful.

Socialism is, in essence, the forced feminization of the populace, placing the populace into a role of female weakness and helplessness to then be protected by the government in the role of male. As such, the men of the Right bristle at, and reject, all socialism, while socialism is cheered by the women and LGBTQs of the Left, and by the men of the Left who feel destined to assume the role of government with its power and authority to protect those women and LGBTQs on their behalf. Any group whose identity and sense of self-esteem comes from being a victim and from projecting self-pity and needing to be protected by someone else, would also naturally fall into the female position of weakness in relation to a male government as protector, and they would naturally support socialism. (The math for self-pity is $Y - N$ to O for Y as Self-Pity, where Y perceives that O owes $+N$ to Y as sympathy but O isn't giving $+N$ to Y to Y's satisfaction. It is similar to other such psychological dynamics, such as loneliness and/or depression as $Y - N$ to O for O owes $+N$ to Y as comfort, or $Y - N$ to O as grouchy moodiness for O owes $+N$ to Y as cheering up.)

Socialism imposes womanhood onto the public, and the socialist government claims the man's role as protector, and so the men of the Right inherently feel that socialism challenges their manhood as individuals and seeks to deny and take away their status as men, which would make them feel weak in relation to their own women and feel unable to fight their battles as men. So the Right will always oppose any position that the Left takes, for government and regulations and policy, and they will oppose them for the sake of opposing them, for the sake of preserving their masculinity, and not because they have a substantive rational objection to why this or that policy will not work, even if, by random chance, the government's position is objectively correct, and opposition is crazy, for that particular political issue. This explains why the Right sometimes takes positions that are crazy: they do so in order to oppose the Left, not because they really care about the issue itself. The Right would favor personal responsibility and, for example, gun ownership or the freedom to run a business, because the men of the Right feel competent to fight their battles themselves, and to win, instead of needing the government to fight their battles for them.

While the Left claims to be progressive on gender, the Left's political gender dynamic is, ultimately, merely a variation of the traditional caveman psychological dynamic, where the caveman government protects the cavewoman public and fights all battles on her behalf.

The Fascism of the Right, is, in essence, the forced masculinization of a society, where an entire nation is put into a state of masculine anger and aggression, and the goal is to dominate all enemies and triumph by conquest. The fascists' goal is to win all fights by means of their –N exceeding the enemy's –N, so they want to be as negative as possible, and their strategy is to engage in any and every fight possible, for this purpose: to strengthen their powers of –N to be as high as possible, because every fight that they win tests, hones, and improves their powers of causing –N. Fascists tend to persecute political dissidents and to punish dissent as Y –N to O, and they also tend to seek out wars of conquest as Y –N to O, as fighting for the sake of fighting, conflict solely for the purpose of making a display of manly, muscular strength. They have no mercy and no sympathy, and they walk the path which, in history, belonged to, for example, the Roman soldier or the Viking warrior, as bloodthirsty conqueror.

In contrast to socialism and fascism, in a libertarian, liberal, free democracy, such as today's United States of America, each individual has the liberty to choose his, her, or their, gender role for themselves, and there is no national gender imposed upon society.

The Right tends to want men in male gender roles and women in female gender roles, because their men and women still rely upon "men being men" in the caveman model, their men need to be men, and their women rely on their men to be men for them, so they become insecure about their gender roles when they face gender-fluidity and their gender is challenged. That explains their love of tradition, it dates back to the caveman dynamic, which, to be fair to the Right, is how humans evolved 10,000 years ago and how we survived until the past century.

The Left is more gender-fluid and LGBTQ, which defines

them as more progressive and modern, because they are more willing to have anyone in any gender role, and they can use women in male roles or men in female roles with success, and so they are less dependent upon men acting out the male gender role in order for their men and women to survive.

Despite the fact that strength and power are Right virtues and softness and sensitivity are Left virtues, Right and Left do not necessarily correlate to Right control/dictatorship and Left freedom/democracy, it is not true that the Right is always dictatorial and the Left is always pro-freedom. Each could be either. The freedom Right are, for example, the libertarians. The dictatorial/control Right are the fascists, who desire total control by a dictator. The dictatorial/control Left are the socialists, the communists, and the progressives, who desire total control by the government. The democracy/freedom Left would be, for example, moderate center-left tax-and-spend liberals. Tyranny is the condition of total control, regardless of whether it is by a Right dictator or by a Left government. In contrast, true freedom requires democracy and civil liberties and a free press, regardless of whether the Left or the Right is the political party that happened to most recently obtain the most votes.

Economic freedom tends to be male freedom, the freedom for the strong: free market capitalism, gun rights, no government control. Social freedom tends to be female freedom, the freedom to be beautiful, or freedom for the weak: things being being nice and polite and being free from rudeness and from offensive behavior, abortion rights, LGBTQ rights, gay marriage, or, as a type of freedom to be weak, protection from racism, the right to use recreational hard drugs, immigration freedoms.

The social Right tends to be, not freedom, but men attacking female freedom, and men oppressing women: preventing women from having abortions, attacking the legal rights of transgender female youth, attacking the freedom to engage in LGBTQ sex or LGBTQ identity, etc. Similarly, the economic Left tends to be, not freedom, but men attacking male freedom on behalf of women, and men oppressing other men, such as men telling other men what they have to do, how they have to behave, forcing people to conform to safety instead of taking risks, and forcing them to obey the government, instead of just letting them do whatever they want.

The Right is masculine, the Left is feminine, and Libertarian is the political non-binary, Libertarians are on the Right on economics and on the Left on social issues.

Envision a grid, where the Right side is male, the Left side is female, the bottom is Collective, and the top is Individual.

Right: Masculine: Collectivist - Fascists, Social Conservatives: Men rule men and women on behalf of men, domination, 100% controlled by men, women are oppressed, (often) a dictator, but economic freedom because that gives men the freedom to use their strength and intelligence, and freedom such as gun rights because that gives men the freedom to engage in physical violence, and freedom to be rude or offensive.

Left: Feminine: Collectivist - Socialism, the Economic Left: Men rule men and women on behalf of women in order to protect women, 100% controlled by men for women, no economic freedom, but (often) social freedom for women's rights, such as freedom from the rude and offensive, freedom for abortion, LGBTQ freedom, etc. There is an emphasis on safety, that the government will protect everyone (weak women) so that no one has to be strong enough to win a fight (as a man), and also the government will force everyone to be nice, polite, and respectful, so that there will be only female beauty, and no male ugliness, that is visible in discourse. They also champion the ideal of equality on the belief that men ruling for women will bring the women up to equal status as men, that the weak and oppressed will be lifted up to the level of the ruling class, by a ruling class that fights for the rights of the weak.

Right: Masculine: Individualist - Far Right Libertarians (Market Anarchists, Anarcho-Capitalists): There is no government, only market anarchy, so there is 100% freedom for men, because there is no government to nag them and whine at them and boss them around and rely on their tax dollars and treat them like an annoying housewife treats her husband. With market anarchy, there is no government to tell a man what to do, so the man has 100% total domination within the sphere of his own individual life, although he loses the fascist domination of men against women, because, absent government, no politics exists at all.

Left: Feminine: Individualist - Moderates and Independents, Liberals on the Center-Left: They want some freedom and so oppose total socialism, and they want some economic freedom, but they are deeply committed in principle to women's freedoms, abortion rights, LGBTQ rights, feminism, equality, and justice, and, in general, they want people to be nice and polite and respectful, and they take offense at the rude and offensive.

A "Non-Binary" is the name for someone who does not accept the gender binary or who does not fit within the gender binary or who adopts both masculine and feminine traits at the same time, or who is transgender and changes back and forth between being a man and being a woman. It is a term used often in the LGBTQ community, although I am the first author to assert that Non-Binary is the gender identity which is expressed in "political gender" as libertarian.

The Libertarian Non-Binary: economic freedom, which is freedom for men to be strong men, plus social freedom, which is freedom for women to be free women, free from oppression. Economic Right + Social Left.

The reason why Libertarianism always fails: Men on the Far Right, who embrace freedom and fall in love with the ideal of libertarian freedom, then realize that the principle of freedom would require freedom not only for men but also for women, as a matter of principle, and then they retreat, in fear of women, afraid of female freedom, and they return to fascism and social conservatism. And the men and women of the Center-Left, who become excited about freedom, that women can be truly free, later realize that the principle of freedom would also require freedom for men to be men, the freedom to be rude and offensive, the freedom to be strong, and so they become afraid of male freedom, and they retreat back to the Left, and have no place to go other than back to socialism. People are too afraid of true freedom because of their gender insecurity, because men can't stand seeing women be free, and women can't stand seeing men be free, so they retreat back into the gender safety of fascism for men and socialism for women.

The Libertarian hypothesis:

The condition of perfect male freedom is free market anarchy with zero government: a set of conditions where there is no government of men on behalf of women to boss around men and tell men what to do.

The condition of perfect female freedom is no oppression, which means, no laws that oppress women.

If there is no government, then there exists no government that can pass any laws, and, if there are no laws, then there are no laws that oppress women or violate women's rights. Under free market anarchy, men are free from government interference, and women are free from government oppression.

Therefore, the condition of perfect masculine freedom, and the condition of perfect feminine freedom, is the same set of conditions, which is equal to perfect freedom.

The anarcho-capitalist Far Right libertarians (known within the movement as the "An-Caps") have a principle, namely, Austrian economics. But the Non-Binary "Economic Right plus Social Left" libertarians, too, have a principle, although it is a different principle. The Non-Binary libertarian principle could be summed up as: "less government, more freedom." Let people do whatever they want.

In general, when the government stops telling people what to do, in economics, the result is behavior that the Right favors. People will trade in free markets, and be capitalists, unless the government forces them to pay taxes and obey regulations. But also, in general, when the government stops telling people what to do, in social policy, the result is behavior that is on the Left: absent government laws enforced by the police that ban the public from doing so, people will do drugs, people will use prostitutes, people will come in across borders from other countries, people will have gay weddings, people will have abortions, etc.

So, if you begin from the principle of "less government, more freedom," then you arrive at a place where your policy positions are economic Right plus social Left.

In general, social conservatives and the social Right are the ones who attack freedom in the social arena, while the economic Left are people who attack freedom in the economic sphere. Therefore, to be a "social Left plus fiscal Right" Non-Binary libertarian (whom we could call by the abbreviation "NBL"), is to be opposed to both the social conservatives and fascists, and to oppose the economic Leftists and socialists, which means, to be opposed to government control and power as such, and to be a defender of liberty.

The economic Right is men being free. The social Right is men dominating women and preventing women from being free.

The social Left is women being free. The economic Left is men, on behalf of and for women, dominating men and preventing men from being free.

So a position that is economic Right plus social Left combines men being free and women being free.

This explains why the Non-Binary libertarian, the NBL, is on both the social Left and the economic Right.

In contrast, the true tyrant dictator would combine the social Right with the economic Left, much as the Nazis did, because the true tyrant desires to oppress and dominate both men and women, and allow neither one to have any degree of freedom.

In theory, along the lines of the gender of politics and the Libertarian as Non-Binary, there could also be a type of Libertarian, on the Left, who is a Libertarian only because they want freedom for women, and freedom for the weak and the oppressed, and they believe anarcho-capitalism is the best system suited to achieve this, and they do not care about men or freedom for men at all, men are not their area of concern. Such people do exist, although they seem to be rare and uncommon.

According to this theory of the gender of politics, a person who was neither on the Left nor on the Right, but who is unique, and is not on the political Left-Right binary at all, would also be a type of Non-Binary Libertarian, because they are not Left and not Right, they are not masc and they are not fem. However, we would expect each such type of person to have their own unique politics, so there would not be one name or word to describe their political identity.

Obviously, a state is the most common form of government, but, even in the condition of anarchy, even in a fully stateless society, I would define the initiation of violent force in order to achieve social, moral, or political goals, as a type of government, and as governing, even if the violence was used only by private individuals against other private individuals. This is why the Libertarian Party asks for a "loyalty oath," that a member will never initiate violence against a non-violent other to achieve social or political goals: because that oath really means you will not govern others. To the libertarian, violent force may be used only for individual self-defense, never to govern other people.

Libertarians often use a visual picture called The Nolan Chart, which is a diamond, with the Right on the right, the Left on the left, Freedom on the top, and Tyranny on the bottom. It is intended to show that Freedom would combine the economic side of the Right with the social side of the Left. It can be updated, using my analysis presented in this essay, merely be adding Masculine to the Right, Feminine to the Left, Collectivist to the bottom, and making the top Individualist.

Some concluding thoughts on these topics:

To be LGBTQ gay: to appreciate the beauty of strength.

To be a feminist: to appreciate the strength of beauty.

As with politics, where a side of Left or Right can have a gender, so, too, a race, as a political class, can also have a gender. We often see a vulnerable or oppressed race move to the Left when it is weak and chooses to be submissive in order to rely on the strength of the government to protect it, and then, once the race has its footing and is stable, the men of that race then move to the Right in order to assert their masculinity.

We saw this in America with the Jews, who used to be on the Left when they were weak but moved to the Right as they became strong, and, more recently, the Latinos have made the same move, the same dance step, they were politically weak and they had been on the Left, but the Latino men are moving to the Right today in order to assert their manhood and masculinity, against what they perceive as a weak, girly, womanly Left.

Interestingly, the men of the Black race seem not to do this; the Black people seem locked in a position of weakness and submitting to the state and relying upon the government for power on the Left side of politics. Black young men (and this is probably merely a false racial stereotype, or it may be true of some Black men but not be true of other Black men) tend to assert their manhood through violence, aggression, sex with women, drug use, gangs and gang-inspired music, daring feats of strength against the police and against authority, etc., instead of through Right-wing politics. There is also a certain type of white young man who copies the Black young man's criminal behaviors in order to assert his own white-young-man's masculinity, by doing drugs and having sex and breaking the law and such, although, being white, he is arrested for it far less frequently than the Black man.

The above is not intended to be racist towards the Black race. This is not intended to describe all Black men, but, instead, it describes a certain type of Black young man who is insecure in his masculinity, because these behaviors are done to assert one's manhood, and to overcome one's masculine insecurity. The math and logic of it is that, when a person breaks the law or defies authority, he is asserting that his negative N against the police and against the government is bigger than their negative N was against him, which is why he won his fight against them. And, when he has sex with a woman, he feels that his negative N was large enough to overcome her negative N against him, that he conquered her by having sex with her.

These behaviors are common in young men of every race, at the age where they are insecure in their masculinity, but, for whatever reason, media and culture tend to focus on this lifestyle among Black young men (and Latino young men, too). Possibly, because historically the Black race and the Latino race were oppressed and conquered by the white race for such a long time, and so they feel that they were dominated in the way that a man dominates a woman, some Black and Latino young men enter the world feeling that their masculinity has already been called into question, so they overcompensate by asserting their manhood in such cheap and easy ways as drugs and crime and gangs. It is all about the size of one's power to inflict negative N, the size of one's masculinity. Obviously there are entire classes of normal middle-class law-abiding Blacks and Latinos who are fully secure in their masculinity (or femininity) and to whom such would not apply, and these people tend to blend in with the moderates and independents of the white race, within the space between Right and Left.

It is also worth speculating that a certain type of political activist or politician feels masculine insecurity due to a history of racial or gender or class oppression against them, and then attacks people with their Leftism and attacks people with their socialism, against what they perceive as the complacent capitalist middle class or their foes on the political Right, in order to assert their negative energy against others to reclaim their lost manhood, by means of politics.

But we see in those rare cases when a Black man does achieve wealth and power, and when he no longer benefits from reliance upon the government for help, he too will move to the political Right in order to assert his masculinity, as, for example, with a very famous and notorious Black man United States Supreme Court Justice on the Right, Clarence Thomas, or else he will assume the white male position of privilege and power in the Left, as for example with America's recent Black President, Barack Obama, who had far more in common with rich white men on the Left than he did with the poor Black man on the streets.

In the United States of America, historically, the white race, in general, seems to be gender-male, and historically the white man had expected white women to submit to men. This explains the Right's fascination with the white race: it is because both of them are gender-masculine in their gender-performance. But people can be racist whether they are on the Right or on the Left. The white men on the Left tend to come to power on the Left, and to rise to the top of the Left, and they are the men who fight for women, they are the men who fight on behalf of those whom they deem weak, they are not themselves gendered as women, they wield negative N for women, not positive N as women. To hold power, and use helping those who are weak as your pretext and propaganda to rule, is certainly not the same thing as actually really being weak yourself. A rich man who donates millions of dollars to charity is not himself a beggar, and he has power and will never suffer as the beggar does; nor is a white man on the Left someone who truly is gender-feminine. He says he fights for them, but he is not them, he has no way to relate to them, it is a pretext to wield power over men on the justification of helping women.

Note here that I define "man" as someone who uses negative N as their survival strategy, and I define "woman" as someone who uses positive N as their survival strategy. I do not intend to refer to men and women by their bodies; here I speak of men and women as gender roles. In practice, sometimes, however, the body, the gender role, and the race, and the politics, will all blur together.

Also note that, while the caveman gender dynamic calls for a man to attack his woman's enemies with his causing –N to them, the man, to be as strong as possible, will fight everyone around him, in order to build toughness and strength, and, so, often the man will attack his woman herself with his –N also, just because she is nearby, even though protecting her in return for her +N to him was the basic premise of their social contract. Thus, man will attack woman's enemies, and man will attack woman at the same time, and this makes sense, from the man's point of view, as agent of –N.

This is why the Black woman leads the most challenging life: she is a woman, and so caveman gender roles define her as weak and submissive and for a man to dominate, and then she is also Black, so racial expressions of gender roles again treat her like the cavewoman gender role.

However, the solution for caveman gender is not for the Left to defeat the Right, as both Left and Right assume this caveman-cavewoman dynamic; the author feels that the Non-Binary Libertarian will emerge as the superior method of achieving gender freedom. The men in power on the Left do not truly desire gender equality, although the Leftist activists and radicals on the streets believe that they do; instead, the men want power, and they think they get more power if they wield it in the name of women and against men, by ruling the economy. But the Right is no better, because they only want freedom for men, and they desire to rule women, and so, despite their rhetoric of freedom, they are no friends of liberty. Only the Non-Binary Libertarians can achieve perfect freedom.

I will conclude this section with this thought, which is that, in perfect socialism, the people have only positive N, however, all their capacity for inflicting negative N is taken by the socialist government, and the government itself then inflicts negative N, on behalf of the people, against all critics and dissidents and rebels. This is why, much as the fascist men in power on the Right will censor or jail or shoot and murder their critics, political dissidents, and rebels, so, too, the socialist men in power on the Left would do the same thing, and cause incredible extreme negative N, despite the fact that their premise is everything being nice and pretty and beautiful and one big happy family of +N for everyone.

+N and −N are inherent in human existence, positive energy and negative energy is inherent in the very fabric of reality itself, in physics and chemistry, so +N and −N will never go away, the only question is which social and political institutions we choose to channel them into a form that we prefer, be they Left, Right, and/or Libertarian.

Insecurity in being a man: Fear that −N isn't big enough for Y −N to O. "I'm not strong enough."

Insecurity in being a woman: Fear that +N isn't big enough for Y +N to O. "I'm not good-looking enough."

Challenge to masculinity: Test of Y −N to O by means of O −N to Y.

Challenge to femininity: Test of Y +N to O by means of competitor or rival's +N to O.

Why adults tend to be more confident than young people: They have survived to adulthood, which proves, mathematically and logically, that the size of their N is big enough for them to survive.

Advertiser and politician manipulation: Subconsciously challenge masculinity or femininity (see above for how this is done), then sell a symbol of boost of Power = –N to men, or sell a symbol of boost of Beauty = +N to women. It doesn't have to be the real thing, what they sell is just a symbol of the thing.

STRATEGIES FOR HOW TO MAKE FRIENDS OR GET A ROMANTIC PARTNER

The ten strategies for obtaining a relationship with someone you like:

Definitions:

Y: You

O: the Other person

+N: Positive energy (as social or emotional value/benefit/capital)

−N: Negative energy (as social or emotional forcefulness/willfulness/dominance)

As: the form that N takes in a particular trade.

For: for the benefit of, for a trade of that in return for this.

(1) Y +N to O as Beauty/Attractiveness (beauty for women, muscles for men, a pretty face, a nice body, a handsome face, beautiful eyes, wearing fancy beautiful clothes, or being good at dancing and partying, or cooking tasty flavorful food for them, or being good at sex. It is the providing of sensations of pleasure to the other person.)

(2) Y +N to O as Speech attractiveness: being funny, clever, witty, enjoyable to talk to, fun to hang out with, being fun to do things with

(3) Y +N to O as Being Nice, polite, friendly, cheerful

(4) Y +N to O as Love (or as a loan of love, such as "falling in love at first sight")

(5) Y –N for O as Assertiveness, Aggressiveness, Confidence

(6) Y +$N to O as Money, buying them gifts, paying for stuff for them, or just giving them money

(7) Y +$N to O as logistical Support, such as letting them crash on your sofa, renting a hotel room for them to hook up with you, running errands for them, letting them share your alcohol cabinet and/or your 420 drawer, etc.

(8) Y –N for O and Y +$N to O as Y Protecting O from danger/risk = N, from either physical danger, emotional danger, bullying, from other people, or from financial danger.

(9) Y –N to Y for O +N to Y, or O +N to Y as Unpaid-for Gift: Present yourself as a victim of unfairness, and ask for O's love out of sympathy and mercy, for them to make you feel better, or ask for love and friendship as an unpaid-for gift, where you give nothing in return. If O takes pride in helping others and in being a nice person, then O +N to O for O +N to Y, so you pay O for O's love by giving O the opportunity to "be a good person" by helping you and being nice to you.

(10) Y –N to Y for O as Presenting yourself as someone who is weak and in need of protection, as someone who needs to be protected and is looking for a protector, and then O –N for Y to Enemies as O +N to Y as Protection completes the relationship. But, normally, what O gets in return for protecting Y is for O to know Y's beauty, so it helps if Y has beauty to "sell" in return for a strong, forceful, dominant, muscular protector to take care of them.

#1 and #10 are the traditional "female" methods of "getting a man to fall in love with you" in caveman gender roles, while #5 and #8 are the traditional "male" methods. #8 is what a man offers to a woman to get her to become his wife, traditionally. #9, in sex, is called "sympathy fucking," and in dating and friendship #9 is called "charity," or "feeling sorry for someone."

The plan is, you do one or more of these, for O +N to Y back to you in return, as a relationship, friendship, love, or fun.

To be loved, love. To get something, give something.

DATING PROFILES

This advice is for dating profiles, but also works for going on dates, and while being in relationships, in general.

Do this:

Y +N to O as friendly, attractive, polite, positive (positive about Y, and positive about O).

Do not do this:

Y –N to O as complain, as you have to deal with my baggage, as negativity.

Y –N to Y for O as self-deprecation, as I apologize for what a bad person I am, as self-criticism, as self-doubt, as negativity.

Always remember: You are trying to make the sale. Your goal is not to lose the sale by being honest about flaws. Trust me, if the flaws are there, they will get noticed. There is no need for you to draw attention to them. Being positive gets results. Negativity drives people away. Also, your hurting yourself and your image for the other person's benefit will not, in fact, make them like you. It just presents yourself more badly than you had to.

WHAT MAKES SOMETHING ENJOYABLE (+N)

The nine affirmations that express +N in such a way as to create an enjoyable experience:

(1) Pleasurable sensations: pleasure, beauty, awe, grandeur, joy, a sense of meaning, stimulation, amusement and entertainment, relaxation, excitement, jokes, humor, music, drama, something that so fully engages the mind that the person ceases to be aware of their problems.

(2) People being nice to them.

(3) A symbol of their self-esteem which affirms their self-esteem as SE+.

(4) A sense of belonging or community.

(5) Feelings that they have done moral good, are appreciated by others, have done right, have been judged worthy.

(6) Seeing O +N to Y through the point of view of someone they can relate to.

(7) Something that matches their unique subjective preferences of what they like (and the absence of what they don't like).

(8) Removal of stress and anxiety, or a symbol of defeating

some symbolic challenge to their self-esteem.

(9) A feeling that they are loved or that they have a friend. This, more than anything, motivates someone to get married and/or start a family.

If you want to motivate self or others to seek to achieve a Goal G, offering them +N of one or more of these forms as a reward is the surest technique for motivation.

CONFIDENCE, OR ARROGANCE

Confidence: Believing in yourself and in your ability to succeed. Giving yourself a loan of self-confidence and trust in yourself.

Y +SE, Y +N to Y as Loan of +N for +SE.

Arrogance: To put someone else down in order to lift yourself up over them, by measuring your self-esteem as your value minus their value, so the less value they have, the higher your (pretense of) self-esteem becomes.

Y −N to O for Y +SE = (Y − O).

Mathematically and logically, confidence and arrogance are two completely different things, although they look the same, and people often confuse the two. The only thing they have in common is that they are both tactics based on increasing one's self-esteem, one's opinion of one's own worth and value.

EARNING VS. ENTITLEMENT

Definition:

For (Y=Y): For who Y is, what Y is, Y's status or title or identity.

Deserving/earning: O +N to Y for Y +N to O as Action.

A sense of entitlement: O +N to Y for Y=Y (because of who Y is or because of what Y is).

Then disdain/condescension is Y –N to O for O –N to Y as O Not +N to Y for (Y = Y). If Y expects to be given +N because Y=Y, then Y feels that O owes +N to Y. So, then, if O doesn't given +N to Y, Y interprets that as O –N to Y. And then Y will give –N back to O for O's perceived –N to Y. And "giving someone attitude" means giving them –N when they expected you to give them +N because of who they are.

IS LOVE A TRADE?

Y +N to O for nothing in return (for Zero) = Y Gifts +N to O.

There is a belief that true love, true friendship, truly being nice to someone, is a gift.

But if someone gives you a gift of this sort, if you are a nice person or a good person, you always want to repay by being nice back, even if the gift was freely given with no expectation that they would get anything back from you.

So, socially:

One way to get everyone to like you,

Is to be nice to everyone,

But expect nothing in return and ask for nothing in return.

Everyone likes kindness and generosity and being friendly to strangers and good cheer and good vibes. If you display those traits, people will tend to like you.

The Charitable Person:

From an overflowing abundance of Y and/or O +N to Y,

Y Gifts +N to O.

If O is a nice, good person, if O is able,

O might, or will, try to repay Gift +N to O with O +N to Y (as Speech, Emotion, or Action).

If O is a mean or petty or insensitive person,

O won't care,

O won't try to repay,

Or O will be negative back.

O Zero to Y or O −N to Y for Y Gift +N to O.

So you make a huge profit by giving lots of gifts away. But this only works if you really mean it. You really intend it as a gift, not in order to get something back in return, not for a purpose of selfish profit. Any socially skilled person can detect your intentions. They will see giving gifts for the purpose of getting people to like you as fake and shallow and evil and manipulative. You have to really intend Y +N to O as a gift.

If you don't really mean lots of Gifts of +N, then fall back on the trade model: Y +N to O as a Loan of Emotional Capital or Social Capital for O +N to Y as ROI (Return on Investment) Profit.

OBJECTIONS TO MY THEORY, AND MY REPLIES

Objection:

Y +N to O for Because it's the right thing to do

O +N to Y as Appreciation for O Likes Y, O esteems Y to be a good person because Y +N to O

But that is not O +N to Y for Y +N to O

If Y +N to O is right, and if Y is a good person, then Y +N to O even if O –N to Y

Reply:

O +N to Y for Y is a good person because Y +N to O.

If Y is a good person, Y +N to O as a Gift, or else Y +N to O is not the right thing to do unless Y owed +N to O or for some other moral reason.

Then, if Y +N to O as a Gift, O +N to Y as Appreciation, that is described accurately by my theory, and if Y +N to O for moral debt from O +N to Y, my theory also describes that.

Objection:

O +N to Y for Because O likes Y, not for Y +N to O

If O dislikes Y, O –N to Y even if Y +N to O

People +/– N to Y Because they like or dislike you, and their liking or disliking you is an irreducible primary that cannot be analyzed or changed, regardless of Y +/– N to O.

Reply:

Yes, I concede that O +N to Y because O likes Y is often the most accurate description of reality, but someone liking you can be analyzed, and, yes, it is difficult to predict who will like you or why they like you, but liking can be adjusted for:

Y +N to O at Time T = Now is the situation, and the condition, that makes it most possible and most likely for O to like Y.

Y +N to O maximizes the potential that O likes Y.

Y +N to O as Y being nice, polite, friendly, respectful, caring, loving towards O, is (usually) a necessary condition, but not a sufficient condition, for O to like Y.

And so: O +N to Y for O likes Y for Y +N to O.

Objection:

True love and true friendship is not a trade of O +N to Y for Y +N to O. It cannot be quantified. Love transcends analysis. Love defies math and logic.

Reply:

No, love absolutely can be analyzed, and it can be quantified. However, love and friendship are not a direct buy-sell trade. I never asserted that. It is a gift, for which you might receive appreciation, or it can be given as a loan, which can be repaid by having a relationship. You can use math and logic to better predict how to maximize the love and friendship in your life. Love and friendship are rational. People, even nice people, to the extent that they are rational, act according to rational self-interest. So if you love someone and you are someone's true friend, it is more likely that they will love you or be your friend, in return. That doesn't mean it was "selfish" in that sense that you were only using them to get a selfish benefit out of them for yourself. If you truly loved them or you were their true friend, you had to have sincere care and concern for them and their well being, for their sake in addition to your own. You should not fake caring about other people, you should mean it. But, yes, all social relationships can be described rationally.

Objection:

Real social reality isn't cut-and-dried enough to quantify with math and logic. It is messy, unpredictable, and emotional.

Reply:

My theory does not purport to be complete. But my theory is an accurate description. It correctly describes a lot of why humans do what they do. Also, emotions, too, can be analyzed using math and logic.

Objection:

In a real relationship, often, you love X, hate X, Y $+N$ to X, Y $-N$ to X, X $-N$ to Y, X $+N$ to Y, all at the same time, and it does not evaluate to a net sum. So math and logic do not describe it.

Reply:

My theory describes this. It's just that my theory has nothing to say about what you should do in a relationship like that, other than to just live it and do what you want with it. I never asserted that all the $+N$ and $-N$ would sum to a net sum, or, if it did, that the net sum would have any special meaning.

Objection:

Forgiveness, moral bankruptcy, as (Y or O) $-N$ to Y, then

Y F(–N) = Zero, then Y +N to (Y or O), describes what to do, but actually doing it in reality is very, very difficult. My system says you should forgive a lot. And then be cheerful, after you got hurt, because you have forgiven the pain. That is hard to do. Very, very tough thing to do. No one could always forgive everything. So nobody can ever always be cheerful and never get angry, 100% of the time.

Reply:

Philosophy doesn't change people's lives. People change people's lives, but philosophy can tell them how to change their lives. Forgiveness is the tactic that could enable you to be cheerful instead of angry, but, yes, you have to actually do it, or else it doesn't work. And it only works for the period of time when you do it, so, if you don't always forgive, then my theory doesn't expect you to always be cheerful and never get angry. You're only human, but that, too, can be forgiven.

Forgiving someone who really hurt you is a lot of hard work. Feeling pain hurts. Forgiving all anger and all annoyances, all the time, is a ton of hard work. For some people, for many people, it might be impossible, especially if their gut reaction, their instinct, is to get angry at people. So being cheerful 100% of the time would be a ton of hard work.

But, in theory, F(–N) = Zero is a way that it could be done. Doing it is the hard part. But forgiveness is the key to being emotionally mature.

I never said my system was easy. It would be difficult to do it perfectly all the time. In reality, I would expect people to use it as much as possible, and get whatever help it provides, but not to use it all the time, not to be 100% perfect and consistent with it. If you aren't cheerful, or you get angry, that is –N, but, later, tomorrow, you can forgive yourself for that –N, too, and ask others to forgive you for any –N you directed at them as anger or sadness or not being cheerful and friendly. Forgiveness is sad, in a way. It means that something bad happened, which is so bad that it needs to be forgiven. But life is tough. My system is a system for living life, as a real human being. If you didn't forgive, you might be angry or resentful all the time, and never be able to be happy.

The theory will make your life better, probably, in certain ways, if you apply it to solve the various problems that it describes. If you do it, it works. Lots of things in life are difficult. Making money is difficult. Diet and exercise for being healthy is difficult. Forgiveness, too, is difficult. But it is the right thing to do. It rewards you with happiness, just as doing the hard work of making money rewards with wealth, or doing the hard work of diet and fitness rewards with health. But this is a realist, practical theory, for using psychology and math and logic to improve your life. It is not an imaginary magical fantasy that you will always be perfectly happy without having to do lots of hard work to use the theory.

ABOUT THE AUTHOR

Russell Hasan

Russell Hasan (pronouns: He, him, his) is a graduate of Vassar College, where his major was philosophy, and he graduated with Honors from the University of Connecticut School of Law, where he was an Editor of the Insurance Law Journal. He is a proud member of the LGBTQ community and an equally proud member of the Libertarian Party. Mr. Hasan has served as a member of the LGBTQ Rights Committee of the New York City Bar Association. He has been a volunteer program leader at the Triangle Community Center, which is the largest LGBTQ community center in southwestern Connecticut. He has also served as Vice Chair and Secretary of the Libertarian Party Affiliate of Fairfield County, Connecticut. He loves coffee and chewing gum, and he enjoys watching sports (Yankees baseball, Giants football, UConn Women's Basketball), comedies, and science fiction/fantasy tv shows and movies. His favorite novels are Atlas Shrugged, The Fountainhead, and Catch-22; his favorite tv show is Friends; and his favorite movies are Star Wars: The Empire Strikes Back and The Matrix.

Mr. Hasan accepts fan mail and questions from readers at this email address:

author.russell.hasan@outlook.com

Bibliography:

Russell Hasan is the author of these books:

NONFICTION ESSAYS:

A System of Legal Logic: Using Aristotle, Ayn Rand, and Analytical Philosophy to Understand the Law, Interpret Cases, and Win in Litigation (A Scholarly Monograph)

Everything is Something: A Philosophical Dialogue About Logic, Language, Words, Meanings, Truth, and The Theory of Things

If P Then Q: Why Philosophy Can Teach You How to Think and Help You Live a Happy Life By the Methods of Applying Logic to Solve the Problems in Your Life and Achieve Success (A Scholarly Monograph)

Moral Logic and Economic Logic: On Knowledge, Choice, Will, Desire, The Moral Ideal, Economics, and Economic Value, with a System of Symbolic Logical Notation

On Moral Psychology and Moral Philosophy: Towards a New Theory of Emotions, Motivations, and Ethics, Using the Insight that Emotions Pay Moral Debts and Moral Credits Owed to Self and Loved Ones (also published under the alternate first edition title: On Forgiveness)

The Power of Objectivism: Ayn Rand and John Galt and Atlas Shrugged and The Morality of Life, Intelligence, Greed, Selfishness, Rationality, Individuality, Integrity, Capitalism, Desire, and Freedom

What They Won't Tell You About Objectivism: Thoughts on the Objectivist Philosophy in the Post-Randian Era

Rand's Axiom Problem: On Objectivity, Ontology, Essence, Epistemology, Deduction, Induction, and the Foundations of

Knowledge

An Essay on Reason and Perception

Golden Rule Libertarianism: A Defense of Freedom in Social, Economic, and Legal Policy

Libertarian Economics: A Manifesto and an Explanation

Economics: A Theory of Capital (also published under the alternate first edition title: XYAB Economics: A GOLD Libertarian Analysis of Money, Trade, and Freedom)

The Ethics and Morality of Human Sexuality

SELF-HELP:

To Be Loved, Love; To Be Liked, Be Nice to People; To Be an Adult, Forgive People: Emotions and Social Interactions, Explained

On Self-Reliance, Self-Esteem, and Intellectual Honesty

Love Without Labels: The Fifteen Questions and Answers that Define Your Gender Identity, Sexual Orientation, and Relationship Status

LAW:

A Law and Economics Approach to Litigation Costs: The Proportionality Test for E-Discovery Law (A Scholarly Monograph)

NONFICTION ANTHOLOGIES:

The Apple of Knowledge: Introducing the Philosophical Scientific Method and Pure Empirical Essential Reasoning

The Collected Essays on Logic of Philosopher Russell Hasan: The Complete System of Hasanian Logic, Presented in a Collection of Seven Essays

The Meaning of Life

MEMOIR:

One Walked into the Spider's Web: A Gay Boy Goes to Vassar

FICTION:

The Paradise Machine: A Science Fiction Adventure Romance Novella, with The Slave Girl: A Fantasy Short Story (Russell's Paradise Found Book One)

The Magic Key Cards: A Science Fiction Thriller Suspense Spy Adventure Conspiracy Theory Comedy (Russell's Paradise Found Book Two)

Fallen Angel and Other Contemporary Coming-of-Age Romance Short Stories (Russell's Paradise Found Book Three)

The Throne War - A Sword & Sorcery LitRPG Dark Fantasy with a Boy Thief, a Knight, a Ninja, a Sorceress, Monsters, an Evil King, and Lots of RPG-Style Combat (The Golden Wand Trilogy Book One)

The Shadow of Heaven - A Sword & Sorcery LitRPG Dark Fantasy with Heroes, Elves, Dragons, Vampires, a Quest, and Lots of RPG-Style Combat (The Golden Wand Trilogy Book Two)

The Castle in the Sky - A Sword & Sorcery LitRPG Dark Fantasy with Gods, a War, and an RPG-Combat-Style Final Battle Between Good and Evil (The Golden Wand Trilogy Book Three)

The Golden Wand Trilogy (omnibus boxed-set edition)

Project Utopia: A Libertarian Science Fiction Anthology

The Office of Heavenly Restitution: A Fantasy Fiction Anthology

The Prince, The Girl and The Revolution: A Science Fiction Fairy Tale

Rob Seablue and The Eye of Tantalus

GAMES:

WARM HAPPY FRIENDLY Core Rulebook, First Edition: The Guessing Game and Trading Game of Supply and Demand